IN SEARCH OF
THE PERFECT PINOT G!

THE TRAVELING GOURMAND SERIES

1. *The Gluten-Free Way: My Way*, by William Maltese & Adrienne Z. Milligan
2. *Back of the Boat Gourmet Cooking: Afloat—Pool-Side—Backyard*, by Bonnie Clark & William Maltese
3. *William Maltese's Wine Taster's Guide #1: Spokane/Pullman Washington Wine Region*, by William Maltese
4. *William Maltese's Wine Taster's Guide #2: In Search of the Perfect Pinot G! Australia's Mornington Peninsula*, by A. B. Gayle & William Maltese
5. *Whole Wheat for Food Storage: Recipes for Unground Wheat*, by Michael R. Collings & Judith Collings

IN SEARCH OF THE PERFECT PINOT G!

AUSTRALIA'S MORNINGTON PENINSULA (WILLIAM MALTESE'S WINE TASTER'S GUIDE #2)

A. B. GAYLE & WILLIAM MALTESE

THE BORGO PRESS
MMXI

IN SEARCH OF THE PERFECT PINOT G!

Copyright © 2011 by William Maltese

FIRST EDITION

Published by Wildside Press LLC

www.wildsidebooks.com

DEDICATION

A.B. GAYLE:

First off, my thanks to William for letting me join the writing team for his awesome

Wine Taster's Diary Series

I could not have written this book without the help of my husband, **Peter**, and the patience and willingness to share their love of the grape shown by all the people we met along the way.

WILLIAM:

To Pinot G wine lovers everywhere.

More specifically, to **A. B. Gayle**, Australia Pinot G lover, without whom this book wouldn't have been written nearly as soon as it was.

CONTENTS

Introduction, by William Maltese 9
Introduction, by A. B. Gayle 13
Warning. 17
Australian Grapes 21
Mornington Peninsula 23
PART ONE: Mornington Peninsula's "Cellar
    Doors" 27
Chapter One: An Identity Crisis Exposed:
    Underground Winemakers 29
Chapter Two: It Starts with the Soil: Seaforth
    Estate 37
Chapter Three: The Alternative Approach: Foxeys
    Hangout 45
Chapter Four: Co-operation: The MPVA and Main
    Ridge Estate. 55
Chapter Five: A Regional Issue: Port Phillip
    Estate/Kooyong Estate 65
Chapter Six: A Culinary Delight: Vines of Red
    Hill 73
Chapter Seven: The Feminine Touch: Darling Park
    Winery 81

Chapter Eight: The Importance of Temperature:
   Ten Minutes by Tractor 87
Chapter Nine: Sculpture: Montalto Winery and
   Olive Grove 93
Chapter Ten: The Past and the Future: Balnarring
   Vineyard/Quealy Wines. 101
Chapter Eleven: The Elephant in the Room:
   T'Gallant 115
Chapter Twelve: Wining and Fine Dining: Red
   Hill Estate. 121
Chapter Thirteen: True Pinotphiles: Rahona
   Valley Vineyard. 129
Chapter Fourteen: The Legend: Dr. George
   Mihaly/Paradigm Hill. 139
Chapter Fifteen: End of Our Mornington
   Peninsula Adventure: Yabby Lake 149
Chapter Sixteen: Home Again, Home
   Again!: A Tasting Banquet 151
PART TWO: Selected Recipes 157
About the Authors 169

INTRODUCTION
by WILLIAM MALTESE

My earliest ongoing long-term relationship with wine was with those bottled by the long-established French châteaux; not so expensive, at the time, that they couldn't be far more easily, physically and monetarily, accessed and enjoyed than they are today. Imbibing Châteaux Lafite-Rothschild, Châteaux Margaux, Châteaux Latour, Châteaux Haut-Brion, Châteaux Mouton-Rothschild, and Châteaux D'Yquem, on the very ancient sites from which their grapes are still grown and harvested, spoiled me for years into thinking that the only really great wines were French wines. That early and long-lasting impression remained with me even as I, my nose, and my palate ventured farther afield with on-site sampling of German Spätburgunder, Muskattrollinger; Italian Valpolicella, Lambrusco, even Frascati whose history goes back 2,000 years to ancient Rome; Spanish Divus, Muruve Crianza; Chilean Cabernet Sauvignon; South African Pinotage and Bordeaux Blend Stellenbosch....

Of course, today I've come to recognize that there are a lot of wines world-wide that can rank equally well with their French Châteaux cousins, and I'm always eager to pass on that good word, along with whatever knowledge of wines I've gleaned, over the years, to anyone interested. Therefore, I was more than ready, willing, and able, when approached by Wildside/Borgo Press to do for them a series of *WILLIAM MALTESE'S WINE TASTER'S DIARY* books, as part of its *"The Traveling Gourmand"* series.

Though I started out with my *WILLIAM MALTESE'S WINE TASTER'S DIARY: SPOKANE/PULLMAN WASHINGTON WINE REGION*, about the wines presently grown in the U.S. area where I was born and raised, I was, even while writing that book making a list to include all of those locales, worldwide, that I figure any wine aficionado might do well (or not) to visit in his or her quest to imbibe a comprehensive sampling of the wines presently offered.

That's why I'm happy to team with fellow writer and wine-enthusiast A. B. Gayle to provide this *WILLIAM MALTESE'S WINE TASTER'S DIARY: IN SEARCH OF THE PERFECT PINOT G! IN AUSTRALIA'S MORNINGTON PENINSULA*—Book Four in *The Traveling Gourmand* series for Wildside/Borgo Press.

A. B.'s travels have taken her from the fjords of Norway to the Southern tip of New Zealand. In between, she's worked in so many different towns she's lost count. She's shoveled shit in cow yards, mustered sheep, been polite to customers, traded insults with politicians, and become an author of romances; along the way, acquiring a genuine fondness, like I, for wines, in general, and for Pinot Gris, Pinot Grigio, and Pinot Griggio in particular.

Originally intending to write a novel set in northern California, about a vineyard being converted to Pinot grapes, A. B. got into contact with me to see if I could give her some background on the production of Gris, Grigio, and Griggio in the southwestern United States. Instead, I persuaded her to look closer to her home for the secrets of that particular grape variety, in that I knew, from wonderful past personal drinking experiences, that some mighty fine wine, of the very type in which she was interested, was found in Australia's Mornington Peninsula area where the cool maritime weather is just what those grapes look for to morph into good wine. And, since the Mornington Peninsula was on my list of destination wine stops every wine connoisseur should visit, I persuaded A.B. to take the invaluable personal on-the-spot notes that have resulted in this informative diary.

Tottom's up! Skoal! Prost! Cheers! Jambo! Salud! Gëzuar! Fisehatak! Genatzt! Gayola! Afiyæt oslun!... *et al.*

NOTE:

All quantities, measurements, and distances have been rendered both in the metric system employed in Australia, and in the system customarily used in the United States.

INTRODUCTION
by A.B. GAYLE

I'm a card-carrying member of Club ABC (Anything But Chardonnay). Given the amount grown and sold, though, I'm obviously in the minority.

Perhaps, I'm just an old-fashioned gal and think that if a wine's going to be aged in wood, it should be red, the richer and more complex the better. If I'm hanging around, waiting for my turn at the tennis courts at night, or in a restaurant where the lights glint in the facets of the crystal glasses, a full-bodied Margaret River Merlot, or a Coonawarra Cabernet Sauvignon, really hits the spot.

However, if I'm out with friends in the middle of the day, the sun is shining, and on my plate is a perfectly-baked quiche, nothing but a white wine will do. One that cleans my palate as I drink, and soothes my throat on the way down, helping me hold up my end of the animated conversation.

After years of scanning wine lists, and saying "no, no, no" to all the Chardonnays offered, sometimes the only thing left for me is an unpredictable Riesling, or the occasional Sauvignon Blanc. At times, I've been so desperate I've ordered a sparkling wine. Thankfully, a friend introduced me to Pinot Gris and Pinot Grigio (or Griggio, as it's sometimes spelled), and I was immediately hooked. At last, here was a white wine I liked. Not too sweet and not too dry. But tracking down Pinot G's isn't easy, and finding good ones is even harder—like trying to find a good man.

Pinot G's, in particular, and wine, in general, continued to interest me so much that I decided to put wine at the central core of a book whose plot-line would revolve around a hero in northern California who wanted to convert his grandparents' vineyard from their traditional Zinfandel over to the Pinot gris variety grapes.

Most people have heard of the Pinot noir variety, but the white wines made from its hybrid variant are less well known.

To make my story authentic, I had to include details about the grape and how it's grown. Then, I had a brain wave; a U.S. author I'd been in contact with, William Maltese, internationally best-selling author of over 180-published books, was actually writing a *WILLIAM MALTESE'S WINE TASTER'S DIARY* series about wineries world-wide. Maybe he could give me some information about Pinot G's made in California.

William got back to me, saying: "Yes, there are some great wineries in California, some producing exceptional Pinot G's, but why don't you look closer to home? Having visited Australia, while writing my novel *DARE TO LOVE IN OZ*, I suggest you start in your own backyard, especially along the Mornington Peninsula in Victoria where Pinots seem to love the cold-weather growing conditions."

In all our travels around Australia, my husband and I had visited a lot of "Cellar Doors". In our twenties, we'd slept in the HR Holden a few nights to save on accommodation during a memorable trip to the Barossa Valley, returning with as much wine as we could carry without damaging the suspension. So, I started by checking out the Mornington Peninsula with its "pristine beaches and spectacular cliff tops, where you can catch a wave, paddle a sea kayak, tackle the fairway at Cape Schanck, or sip a seductive Pinot Noir; a special place where vines thrive in sheltered undulating valleys nurtured by a maritime cool climate that together create elegant, personality-packed award-winning wines."

We packed our golf clubs, tied our double Mirage sea kayak to the roof racks, and headed off.

First, we stopped in Melbourne. Being Sydney residents, we'd always been aware of the inter-city rivalry between these two major Australian cities. Sydney might be the larger, but Melbourne prides itself on being "the cultural capital of the continent". It's famed for its shopping and restaurants, and our brief stopover allowed us to check out its boutiques on Chapel Street, spend one pleasantly sunny Sunday morning meeting up with friends in St Kilda, and finalize our selection of which Peninsula wineries we'd be visiting.

As regards the latter, there was no way we'd be able

to visit them all in one go, nearly sixty with cellar doors. Since only some of them grow, or make, Pinot G's, which was what this wine diary is all about, that narrowed our selection considerably. Our itinerary became even more manageable when we eliminated those Cellar Doors not open to the public during our time there; although the selection expanded, somewhat, when many owners, not officially open, invited us to stop by via special appointment.

Early next morning, armed with a full appointment book, Global Positioning System (GPS), and a guidebook to the area, we headed southward from Melbourne, along the Nepean Highway.

WARNING

Always remember that what's provided for you, here, as but one book, in the Wildside/Borgo Press's *The Traveling Gourmand* series, is WILLIAM MALTESE'S WINE TASTER'S *DIARY,* not WILLIAM MALTESE'S WINE TASTER'S *BIBLE.* Nothing I, or my co-author(s), write is engraved in stone, On High, and delivered up unto you as Gospel which must be obeyed or see you forever damned to hell and fiery brimstone. This book and all *WILLIAM MALTESE DIARY* companion books merely provide hopefully helpful aids for enjoyable wine experiences, much as guidebooks point out certain sites of possible interest. A reader is no more required to agree with opinions offered up, herein, than they need agree that certain ancient ruins are "thoroughly fascinating", rather than "just ugly piles of disintegrating and scattered stone", merely because someone else says so.

Wine tasting is a subjective experience, in that each and every one of us has his own individual sense of sight, smell, and taste. If those were the same for all of us, the chances are good that we'd all enjoy the same wines, and those would be the *only* wines offered up on the market. As it is, though, there are literally thousands of wines to be found on wine-shop shelves; simultaneously enjoyed by some and thought merely rotgut by others. Just because I or my co-authors think a wine looks "luxuriously ruby", smells "wondrously of newly-mown hay", tastes "robustly right to perfectly complement a large, rare, and juicy filet mignon", doesn't mean that you are required to be just as infatuated.

The whole fun of getting involved with wines is to discover what works for you, no matter the thinking of anyone else, including of me and/or of my co-author(s), and, certainly, of anyone, anywhere, any time, who has the audacity to try and convince you that what he or she likes should be liked by you *just because* he or she considers him- or herself an authority on the subject. Don't, for even one second, be cowed by wine snobs who try to keep any enjoyment of wine veiled behind pseudo-mysticism that includes its own arcane terminology like "nose", "legs", "hints of pomegranate, blood-orange zest", "good vintage year, bad vintage year", and "don't dare drink that red wine with chicken!" It all just boils down to what *you* do or don't like, either with one food or another, or when drunk all on its own.

That said, it can be downright daunting to confront the vast array of available wines and try and decide just where to start any wine-tasting adventure. In that regard, sometimes it is nice, to have someone who has "been there and done that" to provide you with hopefully helpful opinions as to what you might or might not expect, whether you agree with those opinions or not.

AUSTRALIAN GRAPES

Australia's first grape vines, from Brazil and the Cape of Good Hope, are reported to have arrived with the British colony's first governor, Captain Arthur Phillip, in 1788. Although wine production initially centered primarily in the continent's coastal regions, around Sydney, settlers gradually expanded to establish vineyards in other regions whose soils, long protected by remoteness from industrialization and disease, proved exceedingly fertile.

1854 saw the first officially recorded export of Australian wine—6,292 litres (1,662 gallons US)—to the United Kingdom. Unfortunately, the same century brought Phylloxera, then decimating European vineyards, to Australian shores; although, strictly enforced quarantine regulations saved some major Australian wine-producing regions, like Barossa Valley, which can now boast some of the oldest vines in the world.

It was overproduction of Australian wine, though, during World War I, that resulted in lowering prices to where several vineyards, unable to compete, went belly up. World War II's critical shortage of beer increased the demand for wine as troops turned to it as an alternative.

Increased immigration to Australia, after the Second World War, brought an influx of people whose long tradition of wine-drinking kept Australian wine production on the rise. The country can now boast a world-renowned reputation for every major wine style, including full-bodied reds, fruity whites, sparkling, dessert, port, and Muscat, with Australian wine exportation to over 100 countries.

MORNINGTON PENINSULA

The Mornington Peninsula has 190 kilometers (120 miles) of coastline, and is only 20 km (12 miles) at its widest point. It has Port Phillip to the west, Western Port to the east, and Bass Strait to the south. In other words, it's almost surrounded by water. If we launched our kayak from the ocean beach at Sorrento, and headed south, we'd end up in Antarctica (provided we didn't hit Tasmania first).

The landscape leading out of Melbourne is flat and featureless. The coastal strip is populated by a succession of bungalows lining the highway and stretching across to the waters of Port Phillip. This is a large bay surrounded by mostly flat land, the far shore only just visible in the distance. Every now and then, a small headland breaks the curve of the shoreline. As the road crests these hills, the water, previously hidden by banksias scrubland, or houses, comes into view. Although the bay is navigable by even the largest container vessels, or cruise ships, over half of the almost circular area is less than 8 meters (26 feet) deep. A long narrow isthmus stretching along the southern section of the Bay almost closes off the Bay completely; its name—

The Rip—attests to the treachery of the area to navigate.

On land, warnings of another danger can be found: signs noting this as an "Elm Leaf Beetle Area". This pest, only discovered in the Mornington Peninsula area in 1989, is gradually spreading north and threatening the elms that were planted long ago by settlers wanting to recreate Northern Hemisphere landscapes among less familiar Australian vegetation. Most of the original scrub that would have covered the Mornington Peninsula has been cleared, leaving lush farmland and an increasing number of vineyards.

The towns dotting the eastern side of the 264-kilometre (165-mile) shoreline are popular tourist destinations for Melburnians who flock there in summer to enjoy the beachside living. The water is safe for swimming and is popular with families whose children enjoy the small waves and long sandy beaches. Further south, the towns of Sorrento and Portsea, straddling the isthmus, have sheltered water on one side and ferocious ocean waves on the other. These are popular destinations for surf board riders, snorkelers, and scuba divers. Here, the water can be dangerous; plaques mark the spot on Cheviot Beach, along the coast from Portsea, where Australia's Prime Minister, Harold Holt, presumably drowned while swimming alone in 1967.

A number of tourist attractions are present to keep holidaymakers entertained: mazes, thermal hot springs, five golf courses, trail rides, an abundance of fine dining, museums, and art galleries. Visits can be timed to avoid or participate in different festivals, starting with January's International Pinot Noir celebration, currently in its fifth year. In June, many wineries participate in the Winter Wine Weekend. The first week of October is designated as Pinot Week with a series of dinners and activities.

In the gaps left between the holiday towns, dairy farms and other semi-rural industries, dot the landscape. Lush grass and fat cows attest to the richness and fertility of the area.

PART ONE
MORNINGTON PENINSULA'S "CELLAR DOORS"

CHAPTER ONE:
AN IDENTITY
CRISIS EXPOSED
UNDERGROUND WINEMAKERS

Cellar Door: Open seven days a week 11:00 A.M. to 5:00 P.M.

Winery Cellar Door Sales: Underground Pinot Grigio, Underground Chardonnay, Underground Sauvignon Blanc, Underground Pinot Noir, NV Moscato Rosé, Offspring Pinot Gris, Underground Rosé, Violets Moscato, Thug Pinot Noir, Cab Merl Oh!, Dr Durif

Slogan: Not everything is Black and White at Underground

Phone: +61 3 9775 4185

Website: ugwine.com.au

Email: undergroundwine@bigpond.com

Directions: 1282 Nepean Highway (Opposite Morning Star Estate) Mt Eliza

After the forty-third set of traffic signals, even though Mt Eliza was just 70 kilometers (44 miles) south of Melbourne, I knew we shouldn't have put all our trust in a GPS for finding our way to Underground Winemakers. Despite our early start, we had a frustratingly slow crawl along the highway, and only just managed to pull into the Cellar Door driveway at 9:00 A.M., our allotted interview time.

Underground Winemakers was first on our to-visit list, and was where our quest would begin in trying to decipher the "real" differences, if any, between Pinot Gris and Pinot Grigio (sometimes spelled Pinot Griggio). "Gris" is French and "griggio" is Italian, for gray, referring to the unusual skin color of the hybrid of the Pinot noir variety from which both Pinot Gris and Pinot Grigio wines are made.

A featured article, "Why Gris or is it Grigio?", by one of Underground Winemakers' owners, Dr Peter Stebbing, notes that even big brand-names in Australian wines seem confused by the gris-grigio conundrum, exhibiting little consistency in naming their wines according to differing characteristics.

"In Italy," Stebbing writes, "the gris/grigio grapes are typically made into a medium bodied savory style of wine. The wine is a pale color; the best ones are structured around a powerful acid backbone with notes of hay, honey, and stone fruit. This is Pinot Grigio. As you might expect, Grigio is an ideal partner to mushroom paste on a warm afternoon.

"In France, Pinot Gris is made from grapes grown mostly in the Alsace region on the border with Germany, situated between the wild Voges Mountains and the Rhine River. These vineyards enjoy a stunning panorama eventually broken by the Swiss Alps. The French wines are big, viscous, and mineral. The palate is balanced with a level of sweetness which might seem out of place in an Australian Pinot Gris; however, when these wines are matched with the rich and gamey local cuisine, the result is sensational."

The Cellar Door for Underground Winemakers is a small corrugated steel building located under picturesque eucalyptus adjoining a small vineyard. We were greeted by a small black cat. After we gave our name and purpose of visit, the feline wandered casually inside and, soon after, Adrian Hennessy appeared.

Adrian and his co-owner, Peter Stebbing, are former employees of T'Gallant winery where they learned wine-making from Kevin McCarthy (a name that would constantly crop up along our journey).

When Underground Winemakers was founded in 2006, they had no other resources than "a number of years of wine industry experience and resourceful hands-on determination". Their vision was and remains simple: "Source the right grapes and make quality, approachable wines which are true to style and expressive of whatever their variety."

The two styles of wine could be understood if referring to wines made in different countries but didn't explain why there would be two different names in Australia. According to Hennessy, there's such a diversity of terrain and climate, even within that small part of Australia, that both Gris and Grigio styles can be made, so getting the right name *is* important.

Apparently, this confusion between the two is a definite barrier to selling Underground Winemakers' Pinot G wine off-shelf in bottle shops, and to landing contracts with distributors.

Stebbing's article blames marketing forces, stating it's not uncommon for wineries to receive requests for some particular wine, with accompanying consumer expectation that the vintners will force grapes into that role, even if the grapes aren't suited. Far better for the winemaker to allow grapes to express themselves and decide their own destiny, rather than have something mandated by vintners who probably can't make it happen anyway.

"Grapes expressing themselves and deciding their own destiny" was a phrase that would crop up time and again during our trip.

"The Grigio is very fruit driven," Hennessy said, "with lots of honey, 12.5% alcohol. The Gris, by comparison, is 'oily'..." To demonstrate what he meant, he poured some of the latter into a glass and swirled it. "See how it's clinging to the sides, leaving a high-tide mark? That means it has 'legs' with 13–13.5% alcohol. We don't try for the full French-style which can sometimes provide an alcohol content as high as 15%."

If you're standing in a bottle shop, and want to be sure the offered Gris or Grigio tastes like it's supposed to, Hennessy says, "look for wines from a winery that makes both styles...like we do. We've selected grapes for each wine according to their points of difference. By the way they're 'female-focused' wines (six girls will drink six bottles over lunch), rather than male-focused (men usually will start with beer, follow up with some wine, then, go back to beer). The palates are different."

Hennessy went on to describe Underground Winemakers' Grigio as "friendly", with more micro-oxidation than some other Grigio wines. He makes no apologies for taking that approach. "Our Pinot Grigio is geared for sales primarily to restaurants and needs to be at its best immediately upon pouring. The last thing I want to hear from a customer is that an Underground Winemakers' Grigio was better to drink the day after it was opened."

If a wine hasn't been aged fully, when it's exposed to the air, some oxidation may take place. That's why some wines are opened and left on the table a while before pouring. Wine takes longer to mature under screw tops than corks, because wines with the latter can't "breathe".

Tony, a representative from JHL Wines, Underground Winemaker's chief wine distributor, arrived and was asked for his opinion about the difference between the two styles. "Pinot Gris," he said, "should be drunk with food. Pinot Grigio should be drunk sitting around talking with friends. The Grigio sells more than the Gris."

Hennessy pointed out that this difference in sales might be because Australian Grigio/Griggio often sells at a much lower price; wines under $20 account for a $15 million total sales in any business year, while wines over $20 account for only $4 million.

Underground Winemakers are typical of a "new breed" of winemakers in that they outsource their grapes from 22 hectares (55 acres) of local vines grown under their supervision to meet their specific winemaking requirements. The small vineyard next to its Cellar Door is more for show.

Hennessy maintains that, on the Peninsula, Pinot gris grapes aren't as hard to grow as Pinot noir. The vines of the latter don't crop as well and are more sensitive to adverse weather conditions. The former are more consistent thanks to the area's maritime climate which moderates temperature extremes.

"Because of the temperament of Pinot noir, production costs can vary anywhere from $4 to $50 a bottle," he said. "However that variety is definitely 'in' at the moment, ever since the film *Sideways* was released." He'd referenced a popular movie based around the travels of Pinot Noir enthusiasts throughout California's grape-growing Napa Valley.

Adrian added, "In the future, we plan to open another cellar door, farther down the peninsula, amongst the other wineries, as there aren't many drop-in visitors where we are. Currently most of our face-to-face interaction with consumers comes from markets, festivals, and tastings. We're also keen supporters of Mornington Peninsula Vignerons Association (MPVA) events at places like the Melbourne galleries and local arts centre."

NOTE: Underground Winemaker's Pinot Gris was

the only local Pinot G on sale at the café we visited in Frankston, a small town on the nearby coast.

Underground Winemakers' on-site advertising can best be described as "edgy", with none of the traditional hushed reverence exhibited by some cellar doors. Among the illustrations on the wall for each wine, many selling for less than $20, was one depicting the Virgin Mary that was tagged "priceless".

Hennessy described the names given to their wines as "states of mind": something for everyone. Though, he does think they've struck a chord with the younger demographic, thanks to Underground Winemakers "Thug" Pinot noir, "Dr Durif", "Cab Merl Oh", and its "Rose-eh!" labels designed by noted Melbourne graphic artist, Ken Cato.

"Some women probably pull up in their expensive cars and feel quite rebellious when they ask for a Thug." Hennessy laughed. "As winemakers, we must continually ask ourselves, 'Who is our consumer?' Since most wines at Dan Murphy's (Australian largest wine retailer) sell in the $12 to $20 range, we once, as an experiment, made a Pinot Gris retailed at $16. We got feedback that we were selling it too cheaply…the quality seemingly more like a $25 bottle." He shrugged.

When we sampled the Underground Winemakers' "Black and White" Pinot Grigio, we found it clean-cut and easily drunk. (It's completely fermented in stainless steel tanks). Their Pinot Gris, matured in old French barrels, hit the backs of our throats with a tad more force. We'd passed some of these wine-filled barrels lined up in the broad sunlight on the lawn in front of the winery to "kick-start the fermentation process".

Underground Winemakers prides itself on being "unencumbered by convention" and is not afraid to use radical techniques in creating drinkable wines "which the average consumer can afford" as their website proudly proclaims.

The cat returned to show us out.

NOTE: For any reader checking Underground Winemakers' webpage, using Mozilla Firefox, be forewarned you may initially end up with just a black page. You need Internet Explorer. In our opinion, the winery isn't doing itself any favors having its site a Powerpoint-created document only viewed from the IE web browser. Of course, having a typo in their email address, on their downloadable order form, doesn't help, either.

We pointed out both web-site problems and was assured they'd be taken care of, but we didn't find any corrections had been made when checking back three months later.

CHAPTER TWO: IT STARTS WITH THE SOIL
SEAFORTH ESTATE

Cellar Door: Open on the first weekend of every month and Public Holidays 11:00 A.M. to 5:00 P.M. or by appointment
Winery Cellar Door Sales: Pinot Noir, Pinot Gris, Chardonnay and Rosé; made solely from Estate-grown fruit
Phone: +61 3 5989 23623
Website: www.seaforthwines.com.au
Email: info@seaforthwines.com.au
Directions: 520 Arthur's Seat Road, Red Hill, on the northern side of the road, next to a section of Arthur's Seat State Park

We headed south toward the coastal town of Dromana, and then turned east to Red Hill and Main Ridge where most of the Peninsula wineries are located. The area south and east of Melbourne is so flat that when terrain contours rise suddenly, as they do, here, the effect is noticeable. Towering above the surrounding landscape, yet only 385 meters (1,260 feet) above sea-level, the road heads into a series of sharp switchbacks to its highest point, Arthur's Seat, named by a Scotsman who saw the resemblance to a hill of the same name in his hometown, Edinburgh.

After stopping at the lookout to enjoy stunning panoramic views over Port Phillip Bay, we set off along Arthur's Seat Road to follow the ridge line. Seaforth Estate is on the left, immediately after a parking area at the edge of Arthur's Seat State Park, and opposite Main Creek Road. If you reach Mornington Flinders Road, you've gone too far.

Coming from the other direction, the entrance is on the right, just after a sharp bend. On Open Days, the owners put out a sign to pinpoint its entrance, but if you're coming by-appointment, on a day it isn't officially open, watch out, because the entrance is completely unmarked.

A huge Monterey pine, standing straight and tall, unbowed by coastal winds as they so often are in California, grows just inside the gate. Clay tennis courts line one side of the wide driveway, and there's a spacious parking area. Once you enter the estate, the land gradually slopes down, and vines run across the slope to the boundaries.

Long before Europeans arrived, this area was occupied by the Boonwurrung who lived in nomadic groups of around thirty people. John Franklin, later Lieutenant Governor of Tasmania, and namesake for the Franklin River, was one of the first Europeans to explore the peninsula. Halfway up the hill, on what is now winery land, he erected a cairn that's still there.

We were met by two dogs that roused themselves from slumbers but soon returned to their don't-bother-us naps. Shortly afterward, our hostess, Venetia Adamson, and her husband, Andrew, ushered us into their house and tasting room.

Like Underground Winemakers, whose website claimed the very nature of Mornington Peninsula was why its wines were so successful, Seaforth Estate expounds that same philosophy, convinced the area's "micro climate and the specific 'terroir' influence the fruit quality and the ultimate wine character and flavor—sense of place."

NOTE: The term terroir comes from the French word *terre,* meaning land. It refers to the length of time fruit is exposed to sunlight, altitude, wind pressure, drainage, and even encompasses soil type.

The area's rich soil is suitable for growing many things other than grapes. Eighteen years ago, Andrew and Venetia purchased the property, at the time a decrepit apple orchard with huge radiata pines, along the fence line, that towered fifty feet above the fully grown eucalyptus in the adjoining State Park. During the first year, they did nothing but demolish and chip the orchard and the pines.

Following a trip to Provence, France, to visit their daughter, the Adamsons visited Burgundy. There, they were captivated by the area and could see similar potential for the land they'd chosen for retirement back home.

Back in Australia, a local winemaker, Kevin McCarthy (remember our previous mention of him?), convinced them to plant Chardonnay. Likewise, he insisted their soil, and the prevailing climate, made the area suitable for Pinot Gris and Pinot Noir.

Not having any prior background in the industry, Venetia and Andrew consulted professionals and read books. They paid particular attention to the little details and nuances that might be missed by others, such as the need to space rows far enough apart, and abut them with "headlands" in which to maneuver and turn the tractor.

A survey laid out 2 hectares (4 acres) for Chardonnay, another 2 hectares (4 acres) for Pinot noir, and .4 hectare (1 acre) for Pinot gris. Each hectare/acre was comprised of twelve rows of vines, two-and-one-half meters (eight-feet) long, planted in north-south alignment, and one-and-one-half meters (five-feet) apart to maximize the benefit of the sun in preventing disease.

For the first twelve years, the owners personally pruned the vines with traditional shears; they've since graduated to French "one-touch-and-cut" power-operated secateurs.

Seaforth Estate soil is volcanic: older basalt; the original surface rock, formed from deep lava flows 40 million years ago, has weathered into the rich burgundy loam that gives the Red Hill district its name. Basalt soil, unlike clay, has good drainage capabilities, but in dry periods needs to be irrigated, here, by bore water.

The heavily wooded State Forest on the winery's border remains a notoriously dangerous fire hazard. The Adamsons worry about the risk, but the Country Fire Authority (CFA) tries to work with all the local growers to ensure controlled burn-offs are timed to minimize any threat to the wine crop. Recently, Andrew made repeated requests that fallen limbs, accumulated on the State Forest's side of the dividing fence, be removed. Eventually, CFA workers turned up with heavy equipment to alleviate at least some of the threat.

In February 2009, a disastrous fire killed 173 people just north of Melbourne and flooded the air with smoke. Even though Seaforth Estate wasn't affected by the fire itself, smoke can taint a grape crop, although the extent sometimes isn't evident until well after bottling. The 2009 fire did just that kind of late damage to Yarra Valley grapes, but, luckily, the fruit of the Seaforth Estate, and the Mornington Peninsula, wasn't affected.

Any extreme weather condition causes concern to growers. Temperatures in the mid-forties Celsius (over 110 degrees Fahrenheit) can occur, and, in summer, heat can be a major problem. To improve air circulation, the Adamsons often carefully remove leaves from the vine canopies (leaf-plucking); although, too much denuding can expose the grapes to debilitating sunburn.

During flowering in November/December, ideal weather conditions are vital, or the tiny, white, delicate flowers can perish, preventing any fruit formation. At the end of 2001, rain and strong winds accounted for an almost complete loss of crop.

We walked one end-of-the-rows section; the dogs, apparently having finally sufficiently napped, joined in. Andrew described his Pinot gris vines as "very gentle, disarming and co-operative, with a small canopy, and lusciously beautiful bunches." Often in late January, even at other times, the canes have to be hedged as the variety has a naturally heavy canopy growth that needs to be reigned in to provide the best possible yield. "The grape likes order," Andrew explained.

Bundled at the end of the rows are large white rolls of the netting used to prevent starlings, little wattle birds, rosellas, and blackbirds, from stealing fruit; although, the birds are known to maneuver their way under the nets. Often, there are non-grape-eating flocks of white or black cockatoos checking in, too, especially if there's a large bush fire up north.

Several minerals are vital to the good health of the vines. These include calcium, which helps neutralize the soil pH levels; iron, essential for photosynthesis; magnesium, an important component of chlorophyll; nitrogen, assimilated in the form of nitrates; phosphates, which encourage root development; and potassium, which improves vine metabolism and assures a healthy crop the next year. Volcanic basalt is rich in calcium, iron, and magnesium with variable amounts of potassium, but estate grape vines are periodically crushed, dried, and analyzed, in a petiole analysis, to pinpoint minerals and/or trace elements that may be lacking and need to be added back to the soil.

At eighty, Andrew still drives the tractor that sprays the herbicide *Basta*—a broad spectrum, non-selective herbicide—that kills off surface weeds.

Since vine root systems need nourishment even while dormant, New Zealand *Mycorrcin* is used to activate indigenous populations of mycorrhizal fungi colonization that negate any deleterious effects of the herbicide on the soil.

Harvesting is conducted very scientifically. Toward that end, crop sugar levels are constantly Baumé tested, with results relayed daily to the wine-maker, because even one day's extra ripening can make a huge difference in the resulting wine. Sometimes different parts of the vineyard are harvested independently, depending upon judged readiness of the grapes.

Since only a small amount of Pinot gris has been planted at Seaforth Estate, its resulting wine usually sells out quickly, even though restricted to local bars and restaurants. Originally partially fermented in French oak casts, stainless steel vats, are currently in use; Andrew maintains there's no difference in resulting quality.

Personally, we found Seaforth Estate Pinot Gris excellent wine; the older definitely smoother, crisper, and showing the benefit of extra ageing.

The Adamsons are understandably proud that noted wine critic, James Halliday, awarded Seaforth Estate five stars for the consistency of its wines.

Winery "Open Days" are popular: visitors taste

wines in the beautiful north-facing dining room, and, especially during the Mornington Peninsula Winter Wine Festival, play **paranaque** (French bocce) on the lawn.

CHAPTER THREE: THE ALTERNATIVE APPROACH
FOXEYS HANGOUT

Cellar Door: Open every weekend and Public Holidays from 11:00 A.M. to 5:00 P.M., or by appointment

Winery Cellar Door Sales: Sparkling Shiraz, Sparkling White, Brut Rosé, Pinot Gris, Rosé, Chardonnay, Pinot Noir, Shiraz, Reserve Chardonnay, Reserve Pinot Noir, Vintage Port, late harvest Pinot Gris

Phone: +61 3 5989 2022

Email: wine@foxeys-hangout.com.au

Website: www.foxeys-hangout.com.au

Directions: 795 White Hill Road (formerly Mornington-Flinders Road), Red Hill, the main road into the Peninsula's scenic hill country, with entrance approximately 1.5 kilometers (1 mile) south of Arthur's Seat Road on the left-hand side

The main building of Foxeys Hangout is a beautifully designed contemporary wooden structure, with huge glass doors, and a spacious deck overlooking a steep natural amphitheatre landscaped with grapevines.

When we arrived, the owners, brothers Michael and Tony Lee, were finishing off a bottling run for Selma of Elan winery which grows Riesling / Gamay / Shiraz / Cabernet / Merlot / and Chardonnay.

Previously, the Lee brothers utilized a contractor with a semi-trailer equipped with a portable bottling line to do their bottling; these days, Tony says, "It's much calmer doing it ourselves and for other wineries." They're no longer forced to rush in order to fit their schedule into someone else's.

We wandered through the dining room and into the tasting area. Since it was a weekday, the former was closed, but its blackboard menu, one of the estate's main attractions, hinted at what we missed.

"Our menu," Tony explained, "is geared to our wines, with a range of light snacks matched to each one." Customers can share dishes with friends. "We can even create a series of bar snacks, or generous 'vigneron's table' lunches, based on individual's wine choices and food preferences. As we use local produce, the choices vary with the seasons, but some favorites, such as mushrooms grilled in vine leaves, and BBQ quail, are always available." Hand-selected cheese and espresso are, also, presented as complements to this winery's much sought-after dessert wines.

Taking advantage of glorious weather, we sat on the deck and sipped Foxeys Hangout Pinot Gris while Tony related how he, at fifteen, spent a week working for Fergusson's Winery in Victoria's Yarra Valley and "got hooked" on wine. Two years later, he was off to South Australia's Roseworthy College to study winemaking, later studying at Charles Sturt University in New South Wales. His aspirations to be a vintner, though, were initially interrupted by his becoming a chef.

It was only in 1997, after his two decades of owning and running one of Melbourne's more popular hospitality businesses, that he joined his brother in planting a 2-hectare (5-acre) vineyard at Merricks North, Mornington Peninsula. They adopted the name of the nearby road—Foxeys—for their label name, and took over as managers of the former Massoni vineyard at Red Hill, then owned by their mentor, the Australian sparkling wine pioneer, Ian Home.

They did additional plantings—Pinot noir on north-facing slopes, and Pinot gris on south-facing (so both would usually ripen at the same time), and Chardonnay—at White Gates, formerly a farming property, now the location of Foxeys Hangout winery and cellar door.

The Lee brothers are influenced by French wineries, specifically the benchmark vintages of France's Champagne region.

Michael believes that Mornington Peninsula has great potential for becoming a prime producer of world-class sparkling wine. He began his career in the corporate world, buying, operating, and renovating popular Melbourne cafes and restaurants in partnership with Tony and their mother, Margaret, including the French restaurants, *Les Halles* and *Garçon*.

The brothers opened one of Melbourne's first "gastropubs" in the early 90's, South Yarra's Argo Hotel, which specialized in Victorian and fine European wines. In 2002, this was sold, allowing Michael and Tony to focus primarily on Foxeys Hangout.

Michael is responsible for Foxeys sparkling winemaking and its unique cellar-door "Make your own Sparkling Blend" program wherein visitors are invited to participate in the final stages of the process, choosing their own levels of sweetness and which variety they'll use as their base blend: Chardonnay or Pinot Noir.

Tony is primarily responsible for the production of Foxeys' still wines, as well as the cooking done for visitors at the cellar-door kitchen.

With his family in residence in a house adjoining the winery, Tony is very much involved with the vineyard day-to-day operation.

While Seaforth Estate's owners, Andrew and Venetia Adamson, are firm believers in fertilizers and sprays, after conducting highly technical tests, Foxeys' Tony believes the best way to achieve healthy soils is to avoid herbicides. "Plants grown in healthy soils will be more resistant to disease," he claims. "There's a naturally occurring fungus in the soil, and insects such as ladybugs and spiders abound. All are eating each other. Spraying can upset the insect population in favor of one bug over another."

Instead of presenting the neat, pristine bare soil seen

at Seaforth, and other vineyards, weeds are allowed to grow under Foxeys' vines. During the four-year transition period, Tony had difficulty getting his head around the concept of a completely biodynamic vineyard, but he never doubted chemicals had negative effects on all growing things, including grapevines.

"While we may be saving money by not having to purchase herbicides," he said, "our labor costs, in keeping the weeds physically under control, have increased." They chop down any weeds that grow over knee level and mow under the vines using specialized mowers. The added cost of that, though, is worth it to them for the health of the soil.

"Anyway, the weeds don't grow into the canopy, so they don't affect the growth of the grape," he said. "If you follow 'organic farming' principles, monocultures are generally not sustainable." However, grapes are a form of monoculture and can live for as much as seventy or eighty years without crop rotation. In a way, allowing weeds to grow lessens the effect of this monoculture.

They don't adopt the practice of planting crops between the vineyard rows in order to provide "green manure" when cut down and left for mulch, as happens in some areas. "We don't need to do that in the Red Hill area," Tony said, "as we have such deep topsoil, with good water retention capacity." Green-manuring tends to happen more when grapes are grown in as little as three to four inches of topsoil over clay, or when the soil is sandy and/or full of pebbles.

The main weeds pulled are thistles, blackberries, nettles, and cape weed. He laughed about the latter, admitting he particularly hates them without really knowing why.

Each year, he thins the grape canopy until it's opened enough to see through. This helps the leaves dry out after rain, preventing mildew. He uses a copper spray and Steiner biodynamic potions.

They do their own pruning in the three-month window after harvest when a convenient opportunity becomes available. "It's one of those jobs that's a good excuse to get outside when the weather is nice."

Do the owners feel threatened by the way big companies have bought into the Peninsula, like Foster's recent acquisition of T'Gallant? "Quite the contrary. It shows the area, as a whole, and wines, like Pinot Gris (for which T'Gallant is noted), are taken seriously."

Tony didn't want to join the Pinot Gris and Pinot Grigio debate, but mentioned a late-harvest Pinot Gris the winery bottled in 2008, from which it made a dessert wine for the winery's restaurant. The Pinot Gris vines were cane cut, leaving the grapes in the vineyard to weather and shrivel, producing a decidedly bright and intense dessert wine.

There has been amazing press response to its Pinot Noirs and Pinot Gris. About fifteen to twenty years ago, the standard of wine generally was good but variable. Every year since 2000, the Mornington Peninsula has produced good vintages. Except 2002, when there were six weeks of continuous rain and self-pollination didn't occur due to "cap-stick". The flowers simply didn't mature into grapes.

"Now, the vineyards and the winemakers are more mature," said Michael who joined us. "Plus, of course, the weather has been kind. After that bad year, we've had seven to eight good years in a row."

The winery was given a four-and-a-half stars rating in the James Halliday 2007 Australian Wine Companion.

Since started eight years ago, the winery has been out to create excellent, yet affordable, examples of the Peninsula's flagship cool-climate varieties. Its reserve range is made from the best barrels and is available exclusively from the Foxeys Hangout cellar door, or directly from the Lee brothers on their website.

Firm advocates of growing the grape that best suits the area, the brothers note how Chardonnay can be grown anywhere, but there are only a few areas where it *should* be grown. Plus, expansion into areas not ideal, are bad for the industry in the long term.

Tony firmly believes that the Pinot Gris varietal has a great future "because we're a small winery, our Pinot Gris production is only 550 dozen bottles, and we intend to stay small. Success for us is selling out our wines each year and making customers wait three months for the next vintage. In the early days, just from noticing our sign, we were getting thirty or forty visitors a day. Now, it's even busier. We didn't plan for this number originally, but, with our background in the hospitality industry, we're able to cope with the demand. Four to five years ago, tourism in the area definitely picked up." It was, as we've mentioned previously, about that time *Sideways,* the oh-so-popular California Napa Valley wine-theme road-trip movie, was released in Australia.

Customers wishing to buy Foxeys Hangout wines should contact the brothers who will direct you to the relevant outlets, or to the restaurants offering their wines on the menus.

Foxeys offers a full range of wines available for tastings every weekend.

Its Pinot Gris has honeysuckle, pear, and hazelnut characteristics, juicy nose, and tight palate. Personally, we found it hit the right spots in our mouths and suspect it's an all-rounder in terms of accompanying food, especially chicken and spicy curries. We've since paired it with our favorite meal of chicken and capers, and found it an excellent match.

The Foxeys late-pick dessert wine was opened at a tasting banquet we held after we returned home (See last chapter), and it proved very popular with our guests, described by them as "very sensual, even better on a second sip". Also, it proved to be an excellent accompaniment to the lemon cheesecake.

NOTE: *FOXEYS HANGOUT,* a book written by Cathy Gowdie, Tony's wife, a journalist, details Tony's job transition from the hospitality business to wine industry. Text, with accompanying photos and recipes, is published by Hardie Grant Books (HGB) and is available in Australian bookstores.

Tony suggested we visit Main Ridge Estate and talk with Nat White (who had, also, been mentioned by Andrew Adamson). "Even though he doesn't make Pinot Gris, he, as one of the first vintners to come here, should be able to give you more background information on how the Mornington Peninsula developed into the wine-growing and tourist area it is today."

CHAPTER FOUR: CO-OPERATION
THE MPVA AND MAIN RIDGE ESTATE

Cellar Door: Open weekdays noon to 4:00 P.M., weekends noon to 5:00 P.M. No buses

Winery Cellar Door Sales: Wild-yeast Pinot Noir, Chardonnay and Merlot

Phone: +61 3 5989 2686

Website: www.mre.com.au

Email: mrestate@mre.com.au

Directions: 80 William Road, Red Hill

The winery approach is down a steep, dirt road, heading south off Arthur's Seat Road, making it unsuitable for buses. Don't let that put you off, though, if you're in a car; your effort to get there will be well worth it. While you're there, take the time to visit Red Hill Cheese on the opposite side of William Road.

The owner/winemaker of Main Ridge, Nat White, started the first commercial winery in the district, concentrating on Pinot Noir and Chardonnay. Plantings at his vineyard began in 1975, and he had his first commercial crop in 1980. His father-in-law, Gwynn Jones, was founding president of the Mornington Peninsula Vigneron Association (MPVA), and Nat was involved right from the start. Both Adrian Hennessy and Tony Lee paid tribute to this co-operative of wine growers and makers, saying it played an important role in their successes.

We were welcomed by Stella, a golden retriever, who should be put on the winery payroll, given the way she sedately escorted us to the door, removing any doubt whatsoever as to the way through the beautiful garden.

The cellar door is an impressive purpose-built brick building which, inside, feels like an English pub. Main Ridge Estate is described by Huon Hooke, Australia's premier wine expert, as: "One of the finest estate wineries in Australia; a seriously good producer. Visiting and tasting from the barrels in Nat's tiny underground cellar is reminiscent of a Burgundy grower's 'cave'." We didn't make it as far as the cellars, but the exposed brick, and warm brown wooden tables and chairs, gave the main reception area a genuinely rustic feel.

We settled down with a drink of Nat's precious Pinot Noir.

Before he was a winemaker, he was a civil engineer; his wife, Rosalie, was a teacher. After retirement, they went on an extended world vacation and didn't regard themselves as wine connoisseurs. In those days, Australia had a pretty limited wine output; most of which was made by either immigrants, in small family vineyards, in the relatively drier areas of South Australia, or by large-scale operations in the Riverina district.

"Our travels took us from Morocco to Scandinavia," Nat said. "We were impressed by the Spanish, Italian, and German wines, but the turning point for us was Burgundy, France. Here, we tasted Pinot Noirs and Chardonnays for the first time. We were exposed to wines made from grapes grown in picturesque rolling countryside. The villages were small, and they were working villages. Everyone in them had specific tasks in the vineyards, and they still do. Potential growing areas are limited by an area's size and by tight planning rules. The best winemakers usually only had 4-5 hectares (10-12 acres) under vine and only used their own grapes. This gave the French winemakers the opportunity to be different, unique. A lesson easily translated to the Mornington Peninsula area with its restricted area for viniculture."

Over the years, Nat worked out that expansion doesn't always result in making more money, so he's happy to stay small and aim for the highest quality. He sees the land on the Mornington Peninsula as too valuable to make bulk wine and Pinot noir as a grape that needs care; areas that don't have the right conditions and try to grow it in bulk shouldn't.

He cited blind-tastings by judges able to distinguish Chardonnays and Pinot Noirs grown in the region because of how the area's excellent growing conditions are reflected in its wines.

How did the Vigneron Association come about? "At the start, everyone worked together on an ad-hoc basis as no one really had any wine making experience but were very keen to learn," Nat said. "Later, with the MPVA, we formalized what we'd already started. You have to take into account that many of us belonged to the generation of baby boomers who travelled overseas, particularly through Europe; we became educated by our travels. This was the era before television and armchair documentaries."

NOTE FROM WILLIAM: Certainly, my personal exposure to wine, and to wine-making, and, thus, to the formulation of my opinions on them, many of which exist to this day, result from my world travels and accompanying exposure to the grapes and wine-producing areas of Europe which existed for literally centuries while pretty much non-existent in the Americas, South Africa, Australia, and New Zealand. In fact, it took me ages to lose my original snobbish opinion that the "only" good wines were those French-chateaux grown and bottled.

Nat White understands the value of co-operation and still works with a small group of his peers, sharing information and experience. What he's learned from life is that the more you give, the more you get back. This is, in fact, the way he believes the Mornington Peninsula area can reach the top of a very competitive industry.

Like the Adamsons, a lot of whose learning was

obtained from sheer observation, consulting experts and reading, Nat also studied, completing the wine science degree via a correspondence course with Wagga Wagga's Charles Sturt University in 1985. "Having a theoretical background helped," he said. "You have to know the rules before you understand the possible effects of breaking them."

He's not fond of jargon like biodynamic/organic/or, even, terroir. He's never going to consult the moon and planets to see when to harvest or prune.

"When we started out in the 1980's and 1990's, one year in five might be disappointing, but this last decade has been good to us and the grapes," he said.

He's happy to have Main Ridge Estate known as a small winery that's recognized for its quality. He makes wine that he likes drinking. Eighty percent of his trade is from mail order or via the cellar door. Fifteen percent of each vintage is sold through restaurants, and only five percent through bottle shops.

In 1990, as a result of over-cropping, he did increase his output and made 800-dozen Pinot Noir, but, "It took me two years to move the stock, as it lacked genuine quality, and I ended up selling it at cost."

Now, he's more careful and aims solely for quality, ensuring that his input of effort is reflected in profit. "You can only build your reputation by the quality of the wine you sell." As a result, blind tastings and wine books have consistently ranked his Pinot Noirs the very best.

As to the biggest threat to the wine industry in the

Mornington Peninsula, Nat cited "climate change", although he does admit that warmer average temperatures likely will initially improve the region's quality. In the long term, he feels some areas that currently grow the grape may actually become too warm for Pinot. He's heard reports from as far away as the Burgundy region of France about growers worried about climate change. They've had too many "hot" vintages, resulting in fruitier wines. "While the temperature may provide a challenge everywhere for Pinot growers, the Mornington Peninsula area is fortunate in that its increased elevation and sea breezes nullify the effect of increased average temperature to some extent."

Also, he's concerned about phylloxera, a vine disease, which so far has not been a problem in the area. One way to prevent it is not to let visitors walk in the vineyards.

"When I was first introduced to white wine, it was 'White Burgundy' with typical dry-strong flavors," Nat said. "Then, I met the great white grape—Chardonnay—and I was converted from ABC (Anything but Chardonnay) to ABC (Always Buy Chardonnay)." Now, the only Chardonnay he drinks is from cool climates, the style of the Peninsula.

Sunday lunch at Main Ridge is served throughout the year. The menu is a la carte, focusing on local specialties and produce from the Estate's extensive organic garden. A typical menu includes smoked trout on a warm salad of leek, fennel, and lime, served with Chardonnay, followed by *insalata di verdura*, a traditional Italian medley of warm winter vegetables, *ciabatta* and *vincotto* dressing. Finally, barbecued chicken wings, or butterflied quail marinated with Moroccan spices, grilled, and served with *orzo risotto*, coriander, parsley, and pine nuts.

The wines we tasted at Main Ridge were superb, but not cheap.

Back at our car, Stella, the winery dog, stared with avid fascination at our roof-secured kayak, as if wanting to ask, "What in the hell is that?"

As we continued driving around the Peninsula, we found vines at different stages of leaf-loss, reflecting different microclimates within an area easily mistaken as homogenous and not nearly as complex as it can be in practice.

Cheryl Lee, current chief executive of the MPVA, has an office in nearby Red Hill South.

"As a group," she said, "the members of the cooperative are carrying on the tradition that Nat and his fellow growers began. They now work with other industry associations such as the Winemakers Federation of Australia, and the Australian Wine & Brandy Corporation."

She believes one factor that makes the association strong is that its original growers were mostly professional people who brought to the table all the expertise they'd gained from their own diverse corporate backgrounds. What started out as basically a social group of friends, sharing information, has become much more. Another advantage is that, unlike many similar wine-industry groupings, this one mixes winemakers and grape growers, and it provides many opportunities for younger winemakers to benefit from, and contribute to, the wealth of knowledge that has been established over the last forty years.

On the Peninsula, over the years, there has been an addition to its original small boutique wineries, to include a few larger corporate businesses. This has brought other changes. Since Fosters purchased T'Gallant, those grapes are sent elsewhere for making into wine. Other winemakers bring grapes in from outside the area, although this is minimal. Not all wineries make their own wines but employ winemakers at other wineries.

"The area has too few larger accommodation venues," Cheryl said. There are 200 bed-and-breakfasts available, none of which can presently house all the guests who may attend a wedding or a conference. There are a few larger ones, like Cape Schanck RACV, or Peppers Moonah Links on the southern coast of the peninsula, or Lindenderry in Red Hill, but the options are few.

We had our base in Sorrento, a half-hour drive at the beginning, another at the ending, of each wine-tasting day, but that was only because we wanted ready access to the sea to launch our kayak.

Certainly, Mornington Peninsula has an abundance of wonderful eateries to keep all kinds of tourists happy.

"Places like the Mornington Peninsula Regional Art

Gallery, also, help to promote the wine," Cheryl said, "as every time there's a new showing, three wineries, on a rotation basis, provide wines for the occasion."

The association's website shows not only which local wineries promote Pinot Gris or Pinot Grigio, but it provides on-line maps that make them easier to find.

CHAPTER FIVE: A REGIONAL ISSUE
PORT PHILLIP ESTATE/ KOOYONG ESTATE

Cellar Door: Open daily 11:00 A.M. to 5:00 P.M.

Wines from both Estates are available: Sauvignon Blanc, Chardonnay, Salasso Rosé, Pinot Noir, Shiraz, Morillon Pinot Noir, Rimage Shiraz and from Kooyong: Clonale Chardonnay, Kooyong Estate Chardonnay, Single Vineyard Chardonnay (Faultline Chardonnay, Farrago Chardonnay), Beurrot Pinot Gris, Massale Pinot Noir, Kooyong Estate Pinot Noir, and Single Vineyard Pinot Noir (Ferrous Pinot Noir, Meres Pinot Noir, Haven Pinot Noir)

Food: Dining Room Restaurant seats 85. Open Wednesday to Sunday for lunch, and Friday and Saturday nights for dinner. A la carte menu is available on weekdays, a fixed price three course menu is available on weekends

Phone: +61 3 5989 4444

Website: www.portphillipestate.com.au

Email: info@portphillipestate.com.au

Directions: 263 Red Hill Road, Red Hill South

Accommodation: One double- and 5 single-bedroom units

From Main Ridge, one the oldest wineries on the Peninsula, run by one of the founders of the MPVA, we went to the largest and newest, in terms of buildings; where the current MPVA President, Sandro Mosele, is chief winemaker.

Surrounded by mounds of native grasses and indigenous spotted gums, the stark-white walled building of Port Phillip Estate/Kooyong Estate is an amazing contrast to the simple shed of Underground Winemaker, to the sunny and comfortable Seaforth Estate, and to the exposed brickwork of Main Ridge. Even Foxeys' architecturally modern design is dwarfed by what's here.

Our appointment was before the winery officially opened to regular visitors, so we pressed the intercom beside the massive wooden doors and were greeted by a disembodied voice. Immediately, we knew we were in for a far different experience than ones that saw us informally shepherded inside by some black kitten, golden retriever, or any other furry animal.

The Cellar Door Manager met us inside the impressive interior.

The building opened in December 2009, after four years of construction. Its owner, Giorgio Gjergja, after decades of running Atco, an electrical manufacturing business, wanted to make a dual statement about the wine he loved and the region that produced it.

Where chooks once roosted in tin sheds, Port

Melbourne architects, Wood/Marsh, created this masterpiece of design and construction that won the Sir Osborn McCutcheon Award for Commercial Architecture at the Victorian Architecture Awards. The jury said the building was like "an archaeological artifact revealed by drifting sands. The rammed-earth walls spiral from the earth and heighten anticipation of what lies below."

The owner's brief to the architects had been: "Build me a truly outstanding and uncompromising architectural landmark; the most exciting new winery in Victoria."

Floor-to-ceiling glass windows provide sweeping panoramas of the vineyards. Western Port can be seen in the distance where it provides the eastern boundary for the Peninsula.

The tasting room's light-filled restaurant opens onto an expansive outdoor deck. On a lower level, state-of-the-art winemaking facilities—a barrel room, bottling line, wine processing plant, cellaring and offices—share space with six luxury suites each with a private deck. The accommodations are very much in demand as part of the winery's wedding packages, and they boast sumptuous king-sized beds, living rooms, and stunning views across the vines to the distant bay. With a discreet "guests-only" entry and car parking, the apartments offer privacy as well as luxury.

With almost half the property under vine, the winery's water needs are significant. However, it tries to keep as environmentally self-sufficient as possible.

Two dams are used for irrigating its vines, and the huge winery roof feeds gravel-filtered rainwater into 500,000-liter (132,000-gallon) storage tanks.

From a distance, the walls look alabaster, but, they're rammed-earth with 8-9% cement and limestone screening. This gives it a much softer appearance than would concrete. The warehouse for the wines has the tallest rammed-earth walls in the Southern hemisphere. One reason construction took so long was that nothing else could happen, which might cause possible vibrations, while the rammed-earth blocks were put into place.

The earthen exterior, with its excellent insulation qualities, and the accompanying wide eaves, shields the interior from afternoon sunshine and avoids extreme fluctuations in temperature that would increase heating and cooling bills. Solar roof panels heat water and additionally help regulate temperature. Low-energy lighting (LED—Light Emitting Diodes) reduces energy consumption by around eighty percent.

A winding staircase, reminiscent of the one in the Sydney Opera House, led to a spotless well-equipped laboratory, and we entered the state-of-the-art bottling facility. Since the bottling phase of winemaking is usually so water intensive, innovative hot air-washing has been installed, here, to conserve water.

Fourteen tanks hold between 8,000 and 25,000 liters (2,000 and 6,500 gallons) of wine. The plant can bottle 4,000 bottles per hour, and it does the bottling of all estate wines, and also wines for other selected producers.

The wine store and barrel rooms are 5 meters (16 feet) below ground and provide a cellar whose humidity and temperature is ideal for wine storage. Old vintage wines are stored in a purpose built museum so the vintner can "vertically test" any current-year crop and compare it to product from prior harvests.

The Port Phillip Estate vineyard consists of 9 hectares (23 acres) of Chardonnay/Pinot Noir/Sauvignon Blanc/Shiraz, mostly planted in 1987. The Pinot Gris (marketed as Beurrot in recognition of the Burgundian name for this variety), is grown at the Kooyong Estate, 53 hectares (130 acres) of vines located in the northern foothills of Red Hill. Kooyong experiences a warmer, drier climate than Port Phillip Estate, and its light, sandy clay soil is also less vigorous than the other's more typical rich loam. The Pinot gris is sourced from the Meres vineyard whose name derives from surrounding water bodies. It has greater exposure to north, west, and east; its soil differs from the other vineyards, with shallower topsoil, and much higher sand content.

Sandro Mosele, Port Phillip Estate/Kooyong Estate's wine-maker, doesn't think that all wines made in the area should taste the same, "but they should all be true to the grape that is grown here." The similarity would then arise because the characters in the fruit are almost the same for most growers due to the similar growing conditions. "Ideally growers should identify what exactly is a Mornington Peninsula Pinot Gris," he said, "then no matter how it's made, it should be able to be identified as such—with its hint of honeysuckle, lychee, and straw: what a Mornington Peninsula Pinot Gris should taste like."

He doesn't include Pinot gris in the same 'A' class of grape as Chardonnay; the latter he sees "a 'noble' grape, in that it can make far more impressive wines from a structural point of view."

A number of people told me Pinot noir is a fickle grape and its wine can vary a lot, depending on seasonal weather. Winemaker, Sandro, though, says, "With Pinot gris, the difference from year to year is not as significant. Instead of calling Pinot noir fickle, I see it more as 'fussy/demanding'. Doing the same tweaking during production, the effects will be much more profound with the noir. For example, the tonnage harvested per hectare is much more critical with noir than it is with gris." Although Pinot Gris is becoming more popular, he sees Sauvignon Blanc as a good "entry level" wine to translate non-wine drinkers into wine drinkers; Pinot Gris the *next* logical step.

"The emphasis on whether a white wine is wooded or not gives people, particularly novice wine drinkers, the wrong expectation," he maintains. "I barrel-ferment my Gris for textural, not taste reasons. The oxidation process is to express certain characteristics and suppress others." He's out to express the minerality and make it less about the fruit.

Pinot Noir is the winery's biggest export, making up 60-70% of its production. The Kooyong Beurrot Pinot

Gris is so popular that there was none for us to taste at the winery. We purchased one there, which was lucky, as we were hard-pressed to find even one bottle in any local retail outlet.

"It's all about the right variety in the right region," Sandro stressed. "Australia should have distinctive regions with the wines produced in each area being 'regionally expressive'. The Mornington Peninsula area is indebted to the fact that Kathleen Quealy and Kevin McCarthy wanted to do something different and were fortunate the grape variety they picked, Pinot gris, suited the region. Calling a wine region 'south-east Australia' is dumbing it down. Each area should do what it's good at. For the Mornington Peninsula, it's Pinot Noir/Chardonnay/Pinot Gris and some Shiraz."

We left as the Melbourne Ladies Luncheon group arrived to feast on St. Helen's oysters with a cucumber sorbet; demitasse of parsnip soup, white truffle oil; summer crab fillets and lemon aioli.

NOTE: The winery hosts special events. The 2010 "Truffle Dinner", held mid-August, featured Peter Cooper, who established Perigord Truffles of Tasmania in 1993. Some of his prized Perigord truffles were used by Chef Simon West to create a gourmet-delight menu whose every course was matched by one of the Estate wines.

Looking back, as we left, the building's white walls reminded me of the curve a bow-wave creates, much like Giorgio Gjergja's yacht, *Ausmaid,* would have made, in 1996, when it won the prestigious Sydney-to-Hobart yacht race.

CHAPTER SIX: A CULINARY DELIGHT
VINES OF RED HILL

Restaurant: Open 11:00 A.M. to 5:00 P.M. for lunch: Tuesday to Sunday. Dinner: Friday and Saturday

Winter trading: Wednesday to Sunday and from 6:30 P.M. Friday and Saturday

Brunch every Sunday from 10:30 A.M.

Wines available with meal unless sold out: 100% Estate grown Pinot Noir, Pinot Gris, Chardonnay and a unique Cold Climate Gewurztraminer

Phone: +61 3 5989 2977

Website: www.vinesofredhill.com.au

Email: info@vinesofredhill.com.au

Directions: 150 Red Hill Road, Red Hill

Vines at Red Hill is not a commercial winery, *per se*. Rather, under the watchful eye of Bellarine-Peninsula winemaker, Robin Brockett, its grapes are turned into quality wines available *only* at the Cellar Door and the restaurant.

The restaurant is easy to find, just a short drive down the road from Port Phillip Estate, past the entrance to

Darling Park winery. Once again, the architecture is different from what we'd already seen. Its pink cement rendering, with grey roof and trimming, gives it a decidedly Mediterranean feel.

While no dog or cat was there to greet us, the well laid-out garden, with paths hedged in with lavender, under huge eucalyptus trees, created a welcoming atmosphere. The dining room was decidedly warm and friendly, with its large windows that overlook a large portion of the 8-hectare (21-acre) estate.

The vineyard, planted in 1998, includes Pinot noir, Pinot gris, Chardonnay, and some Gewurztraminer.

The Pinot Noirs are aged in French oak for twelve months. The Chardonnay undergoes six-month maturation, and lees-fermentation, in stainless steel. Vines of Red Hill is one of the few places on the Peninsula with Gewurtztraminer. This is grown as a dessert wine and is fermented in seasoned French oak, left to mature in lees for three months, and, then, aged further in seasoned oak.

NOTE: Lees refer to deposits of dead yeast, or residual yeast, and/or other particles, that precipitate, and/or are carried, by the action of "fining", to the bottom of a vat of wine after fermentation and aging. Normally, the wine is, then, transferred to another container, leaving this sediment behind. Some wines are 78aged for a time on the lees, leading to distinctive yeasty aromas and tastes. The lees may even be stirred to promote uptake of the lees' flavor.

Chef James Redfern was holding the hands-on cooking class of every third Wednesday of every month. Before the end of May, the classes had been fully booked to the end of the year, the result of people more educated, these days, about wine and food, because of popular television programs like "Masterchef".

That day, the class prepared marinated and fried leatherjacket with an egg dressing; calamari grilled with sweet and sour peppers and pickled cherries; seared Tommy Ruff; and a duo of spatchcock with wheat semolina and verjuice glaze. Dessert was a mix of chocolate, meringue, and blood oranges.

Although James has only been at Vines since 2007, he spent four years as the head chef of another Mornington Peninsula restaurant (Montalto Vineyard and Olive Grove). The Vines' restaurant manager, Russell Bald, and he worked together at the iconic century-old Italian restaurant Florentinos in Melbourne.

James is a firm advocate of *"La cuisine spontanée"*, as espoused by the late Frédy Girardet, the legendary chef who believed fresh food markets provide all the daily inspiration a chef needs. All the Vines of Red Hill restaurant produce is bio-dynamically grown on nearby French Island. A number of artisan-producers in the area supply every other thing the restaurant needs, from hand-made cheeses to aged cherry balsamic vinegar.

Every Sunday, from 10:30 A.M., guests are invited to "wander down and relax with the paper", and are greeted with a Red Hill Sunrise non-alcoholic drink created from local fruit juices, followed by a leisurely brunch-style menu that highlights the season's local gems. Children are welcome and are served a simplified version of the day's menu.

Even though there are now sixty wineries with restaurants in the area, compared to only eight or nine a few years ago, business at Vines of Red Hill has picked up, because there are now more people venturing to its end of Red Hill Road. The East-Link bypass has been completed, and more people now come from East Melbourne, only an hour's drive away.

Pinot Gris is the most popular white on its wine list. So much so that the restaurant had already sold out of its latest vintage and served us the Pinot Gris from the Darling Park winery next door.

We were amused by the sudden eaves-dropped conversation at an adjoining table with newly-arrived diners.

"What would you like to drink with your meal, Ma'am? Chardonnay?" the waiter asked.

"I don't like Chardonnay."

"What about a Pinot Gris, then?"

"Yes, please."

We asked Russell why white wines, served straight from the refrigerator, have almost a tart taste that never seems present when sampled at cellar doors.

He explained that chilling can mask flavors; therefore, wine "shouldn't be drunk straight from the fridge." Most times, in tasting places, the wine is on the bench and at room temperature. Of course, Russell was talking room temperatures "in southern Victoria", not in a pub in "Oodnadatta" in the hot, dry Australian outback.

NOTE: Other wine makers recommend only refrigerating white wine to 10 degrees Celsius (50 degrees Fahrenheit) just before serving. Chill it any longer and you "risk losing the flavors and structure."

Our meal consisted of my carrot tortellini and my partner's terrine. Main courses on offer included King George Whiting, grilled and served with greens and cauliflower beignets; Bass Strait Groper (a type of Wrasse), slow roasted with creamed potatoes and sticky mushrooms; grass-fed Wagyu rump, spiced spinach, parfait and a classic Hermitage sauce; marinated rare duck breast with beet relish, puy lentils and glazed turnips. All, of course, served with wine. By way of dessert, we were treated to the chocolate, meringue, and blood oranges, prepared by that day's cooking class.

The restaurant is open Fridays to Sundays for dinner. A dinner menu might include appetizers of scallop tortellini with capers, roasted sweet pepper, olives and sage; partridge terrine with sweet and sour rhubarb; Red Hill cherry balsamic and house brioche toasted; a tasting board for two consisting of house made charcutiere, duck neck sausage, potted rabbit, partridge pate, game parfait and truffled broccoli dip, with pickles, and toast. Sweets could well consist of a Shelley's carmelized lemon tart with citrus compote and ice cream;

tamarillo gratin with peppermint and Mascarpone; persimmon and ginger pudding with sauce suzette and house cream. There are daily selections of petite fours and treats, from local artisan cheese maker, Trevor Brandon, that are served with dates, toasted house brioche, and crackers.

As the restaurant seats eighty people, and its adjoining terrace can accommodate 120 for cocktails, it's a popular venue for weddings and corporate events.

There's the alternative Tower Suite, created for special celebrations, or dinner parties for groups of up to twelve people. Modern art sets the style, here, with Villeroy and Boch crockery, and Riedel stemware. Private access assures discretion and privacy.

There are four luxury rooms for overnight accommodation called "Kudos at the Vines".

In the surrounding townships, there are smaller eateries, like the Long Table Restaurant in Red Hill South, which offers a seasonal menu, accompanied by local and imported wines. Located just near the MPVA office is the Red Hill Bakery / Café which offers sourdough, Turkish, ciabatta, and its unique wine bread baked on a stone-oven floor; its pastries are trans-fat free; the gourmet pie fillings are slowly braised, then oven-roasted; its handmade cakes are all made on the premises.

The Red Hill Caterers Café and Store, located opposite the school at Main Ridge, has a wide selection of hand-made pastas, as well as curries, plus beef-and-burgundy, chicken-and-mushroom pies. All of which, including their desserts, cakes and muffins, are made on-site, using eggs from free-ranging chickens.

Area stores offer a wide range of produce, from around the world, including local and overseas wine, enabling visitors to stock up, find a comfortable rest stop, and enjoy the fabulous view while dining al fresco.

CHAPTER SEVEN: THE FEMININE TOUCH
DARLING PARK WINERY

Cellar Door: Open every day 11:00 A.M. to 5:00 P.M.
Café open for lunch Saturdays and Sundays noon to 4:00 P.M.
Cellar door: Sparkling Rosé, Sparkling Pinot Noir, Pinot Gris, Pinot Gris/Viognier, Viognier, Chardonnay, Reserve Chardonnay, Rosé, Pinot Noir, Shiraz, Cane-cut Pinot Gris
Phone: +61 3 5989 2324
Website: www.darlingparkwinery.com
Email: wine@darlingparkwinery.com
Directions: 232 Red Hill Road, Red Hill

This winery, right next door to Vines of Red Hill, and only a short drive away from Port Phillip Estate, was established in 1989, and has, since, been granted a 5-star rating by Australian wine expert James Halliday.

Originally, as a mom-and-pop operation, "Sarge" and Dely Sargeant planted vines, made the initial wine, staffed the cellar door, made marvelous tarts, flambées, and charmed one and all.

With Sarge's passing and Delys' retirement, the winery passed into the hands of the Liberman and Coe families that took Darling Park into new growth.

Winemaker Judy Gifford joined the business after completing formal training at the University of Burgundy, France, and being employed by some of Mornington Peninsula's best labels, including Dromana Estate.

One of her most important skills, she believes, is her ability to gain the most from grapes in order to craft wines with personality and style. "Fruit quality and fruit character," she said, "determine 90% of the result. That is, the better the fruit (health and ripeness mainly), the better the wine—in principle. As for character, personality—the climate, weather, aspect, soils, trellising, pruning, crop level, clone, and an endless range of other factors, make their contribution."

Because she got her degree in France, her winemaking tends to be Alsatian, with her belief that any wine should be true to its terroir—low crops, organic, and sustainable growing regimes, indigenous yeasts, moderate use of oak, and generally fairly traditional (aka French-influenced modern-Australian) winery practices. Of course, she, also, includes more than a little "Taoism" by aiming toward producing the best possible wines from land and vines available. "Our viticulture practices," she says, "ensure that only minimal amounts of sprays are used to control pests and disease, with our aim to be shortly 'certified organic'. We haven't used any herbicides or pesticides at the home vineyard since mid 2006."

Grapes are sourced partially from the winery's 1.4-hectare (3.5-acre home vineyard in Red Hill which, planted in 1989, is constantly upgraded and modified as part of an endless quest for better fruit. Additional grapes come from vineyards with proven track records for producing superior quality fruit, like from retired-medico Hugh Robinson's vineyard in Moorooduc, a warmer site at a 50-meter (165-foot) altitude. It grows Pinot noir, Chardonnay, Pinot gris, Viognier, and Shiraz by-the-.4-hectare (1-acre) and not by the more common by-the-ton basis. More Pinot noir grapes (three clones: 115, MV6 and 777) come from a block planted off McIlroys Road, just around the corner from Darling Park's cellar door, at a 150-meter (500-foot) altitude, on a due-north slope. The Pinot gris is sourced from the eastern side of Red Hill Road, and, most recently, grapes from Graham and Dorothy Turner of Kings Creek, Balnarring.

Originally, Darling Park's Pinot Gris was a "classic" dry, later it was presented as a 50-50 blend with Vognier, but, as well as returning to the single varietal, Judy wanted a late-harvest, cane-cut style, and has pretty much managed one every year since her arrival. Cane-cut vines are left with their fruit hanging until sugars are high enough to pick for "sticky wine". It is, then, wild-fermented, using natural indigenous yeast, in mature oak barrels (or often, "barrel", singular, in that production seldom exceeds 250-400 liters [60-100 gallons], in 375-ml. [13-oz.] bottles, in any given year).

NOTE: As for Viognier, on its very own, ever gaining prime importance in the Australian market, Judy doubts it'll ever happen, if just because, "Australians are reluctant to buy a wine they can't pronounce."

Darling Park's labels are well known for their beautiful artwork, initially using romantic Rubenesque images, then details from paintings in the Wallace Collection, and, more recently, from the artwork of modern Australian artists Arthur Boyd, John Olsen, Sidney Nolan, John Percival, and Charles Blackman that are part of the Liberman's personal collection.

The Café at Darling Park is open for lunch on Saturday and Sundays for delicious regional, seasonal platters, and light meals from local produce. There's always a hot dish, too— maybe lamb-shoulder hotpot, or spicy meatballs, perfect with a glass of Darling Park wine. Also, available are picnic hampers, each complete with a rug, to enjoy quiet spots amongst the vines. (Nat White, with his fear of phylloxera, might not approve.)

Darling Park caters for wedding ceremonies and receptions, special birthday parties, and corporate functions. Its cellar door can book as many as fifty simultaneous guests; vineyard marquees can handle even larger groups.

Apart from the cellar door, and online (with a small freight fee for most deliveries in Australia), Darling Park wines are available from several bottle shops in Sydney and Melbourne. A number of wines are also available at their next-door vineyard / restaurant,

Vines of Red Hill. The Pinot Gris we drank there was a perfect accompaniment to our cold lunch-time meal, perfectly complementing our pasta, terrine and dessert.

CHAPTER EIGHT: THE IMPORTANCE OF TEMPERATURE
TEN MINUTES BY TRACTOR

Cellar Door: Open daily 11:00 A.M. to 5:00 P.M.

Restaurant: Wednesday to Sunday for lunch and Thursday to Saturday for dinner

Wines at the Cellar Door: Pinot Noir and Chardonnay (both single vineyard and winery blends), Sauvignon Blanc, Pinot Gris, Tempranillo

Phone: +61 3 5989 6080

Website: www.tenminutesbytractor.com.au

Email: info@tenminutesbytractor.com.au

Directions: 1333 Mornington-Flinders Road, Main Ridge

We'd been warned that Dr. Martin Spedding, the driving force behind Ten Minutes by Tractor, having taken it over from its three founding families in early 2004, was overseas. Undeterred, we stopped at the cellar door to sample its Pinot Grigio, and a male attendant poured us some wine, answered some basic questions and, then, pretty much ignored us; or, maybe, we just "thought ourselves ignored", having been so spoiled by the undivided attention of friendly pets, managers, and owners at other wineries happier to share with us their love of the grape and the wine they made.

Luckily, we already knew Ten Minutes by Tractor took a non-interventionist approach to its winemaking, adopting traditional techniques that helped enhance flavors, complexity, elegance, and length of its wines, allowing them to ferment via indigenous or "wild" yeasts residing naturally in the vineyard and on the skins of its grapes.

Actually, its three vineyards are ten minutes apart by tractor (thus, the winery's name). The McCutcheon, Wallis, and Judd, are all within the Main Ridge sub-region, one of the coolest and highest parts of the Mornington Peninsula. Pinot noir and Chardonnay are grown on all three, while Pinot gris and Tempranillo grow in the Wallis, and Sauvignon blanc in the Judd.

All three include vertical shoot positioning (VSP), Scott-Henry trellis systems, and viticultural practices, such as leaf plucking, hedging, bunch thinning, and harvesting, done by hand. The blocks are picked and vinified separately, allowing the maximum flexibility prior to bottling, thus enabling the winemaker to identify the best performers for release as single vineyard wines, and/or for inclusion in the best blends.

Labeling and bottling takes into account in which vineyard, or vineyards, the grapes are grown; "10X" designates the contents as a combination of fruit from all three.

Pinot Noir is aged for 12 to 18 months in French oak barriques and lightly "fined".

NOTE: Fining agents, usually, are forms of protein used to improve quality by removing excess or undesired levels of phenolics from a wine. Phenolics are found in the skins and seeds of grapes and are important for structure and mouth-feel in wine, although they can also contribute to the browning of white wines, along with the production of "hard" bitter aftertastes. Free-run juice typically contains very low levels of phenolics as it has not been in contact with skins or seeds for any length of time. If a second pressing is done, the level of phenolics will rise. Fining agents are typically naturally occurring proteins, or substances, that have been synthesized to mimic the action of proteins. As phenolic substances have a strong natural chemical affinity for proteins when they come in contact with each other, they react, and precipitate out of the wine or juice. This is why, on many labels, they commonly list such substances as gelatine, milk solids, egg whites and Isinglass which is prepared from the swim bladders of certain fish.

Chardonnay, Pinot Gris, and Sauvignon Blanc are barrel-fermented in French-oak. All wines are bottled under screw-caps to prevent cork taint, random oxidation, and preserve pristine characters.

NOTE: During a couple of the region's annual Winter Wine Weekends, the assistant winemaker ran interactive master-classes on wine making. Those who attended described them as the "best wine-tasting experiences ever had". The classes looked at wine from the winemaker's perspective, focusing on the differences between stainless steel and oak fermentations, and looking at key clones of Pinot noir from which a sample wine was made and blended to taste.

The website has comprehensive information in archived newsletters, including articles describing how temperature fluctuations, even in a small area, can produce disparate ripening times, enabling "single vineyard" wines which reflect these differences.

Ten Minutes by Tractor's restaurant is under the watchful eye of Chef Stuart Bell. Its a la carte menu can include smoked eel consommé with eel custard, flathead, and sea scallop; confit of ocean trout, Echuca yabbies, braised leek, cauliflower; pressed terrine of quail, mushroom, celeriac, red quinoa, shallot, and hazelnut dressing; partridge breast, chestnut tagliolini, ham hock, pumpkin, rosemary velouté; pot au feu of poached rabbit loin, tortellini; spice roasted duck breast, celeriac, lentils, pear, truffle oil; venison with buckwheat polenta, pancetta, brussel sprouts, port, and fig jus; and Cape Grim beef fillet, beef cheek and horseradish croquette, red wine jus.

Our bottle of Pinot Gris, impressed us by how well it teamed with "Bushranger Gold", a soft washed-rind cheese from the local Red Hill Cheese factory.

NOTE: For a time, eccentrically, the winery professed a relationship between its wines and music. Its website suggested its Pinot noir loved romantic or sexy music, such as Mozart's *Eine Kleine Nachtmusik*, but clashed with polkas; its oaky Chardonnay needed something sultry and tasted best with "blues", such as Ella Fitzgerald's *St. Louis Blues*, but clashed with light, cheery music.

CHAPTER NINE: SCULPTURE
MONTALTO WINERY AND OLIVE GROVE

Cellar Door: Open daily from 11:00 A.M. to 5:00 P.M.

Restaurant: Rating a "Chef's One Hat" from *The Age* Newspaper. Open for lunch daily noon to 3:00 P.M., dinner Friday & Saturday 6:30-11:00 P.M. (during winter) and Monday to Thursday 6:00 P.M. to 9:00 P.M. in summer

The Piazza: Open weekends from noon in winter, daily from 11:00 A.M. in summer

Picnics may be held in the garden October-April daily from noon

Closed Christmas Day

Wines at Cellar Door: 100% Estate grown Pinot Noir, Pinot Grigio, Sauvignon Blanc/Semillon, Chardonnay, Rosé, Shiraz, and a late harvest Riesling marketed under the Pennon Hill range and Riesling, Chardonnay, Pinot Noir and Cuvee One under the Montalto range and a no alcohol Pinot Noir, called Montalto "Verj"

Phone: +61 3 5989 8412

Website: www.montalto.com.au
Email: Use the contact form on their website
Directions: 33 Shoreham Road, Red Hill South

Montalto Winery and Olive Grove is on the south-eastern side of the region, situated next to the famous Tuck's Ridge estate and only minutes from the town of Shoreham, on the banks of the eastern waterway, Western Port, bordering the Mornington Peninsula.

Noticeable upon arrival are two sculptures. One is tall and fascinatingly metal-shaped. The other is intriguingly of green Astroturf. The latter is identified in an attending plaque as: *Clip* by Sebastian di Mauro, developed from his body of work, *Floccus*, exploring the close relationship between people and nature, while alluding to Australia's time-honored weekend pastime of lawn-mowing and topiary in pursuit of manicured, formal grounds. Imbued with humor influenced by Australians' ironic attitude, it encourages laughter in an indulgent yet self-depreciating way whilst bringing into question some of the more curious, yet inexplicable, realities of everyday life.

It has been the desire of owners, John and Wendy Mitchell, from the get-go, to combine their passion for art with their love of nature and growth. The Montalto sculpture collection includes works by Andrew Rogers, Jason Waterhouse, Michael Needham and David Waters. In addition to direct acquisitions, the collection grows by virtue of an annual Montalto competition which is open to artists working in any medium. A $20,000 prize is awarded by an expert judging panel, and the winning sculpture takes its pride of place among previous winners at the vineyard. Also, there's a People's Choice Award of $1,000.

Area landscaping was inspired by how the local geography slopes toward the sea, reminiscent of French vineyards seen by John and Wendy in the 1980s.

Boardwalks allow visitors to appreciate natural wetlands created by four spring-fed dams linked by a stream through the valley floor of the amphitheatre-shaped property. Over ninety species of native bird and animal life inhabit the area. An ongoing program for additional planting will hopefully improve the ecology even more, and encourage even more native plant and wildlife.

The Mitchells see themselves as caretakers of the land, nurturing the best out of it, not pushing or demanding results, but, instead, using it in a sustainable manner, recognizing its particular characteristics, and sharing its wonderful attributes with others.

At the main building, we were made welcome with white figs from Wendy, as she passed through on her way to the restaurant kitchen from the winery's extensive garden. The figs, teamed with local cheese, and a glass of Montalto Pinot Grigio, were a perfect combination.

To ensure fresh, seasonal produce for the restaurant's menu, Wendy created and tends the garden which organically grows heirloom herbs, vegetable varieties, strawberries, raspberries, and loganberries. Orchards provide figs, stone fruit, almonds, hazelnuts, citrus, and olives. The latter play a particular role in the "Montalto experience", in that, every mid-July, there's the Montalto Vineyard and Olive Grove Abundance Festival that celebrates the olive harvest. Market stalls are set up so visitors see, smell, touch and taste their way from freshly pressed olive oil to cooking demonstrations. Visitors learn about olive cultivation and can buy the best varieties for their own gardens from the Montalto's olive-tree nursery. There are even olive-oil massages.

John became hooked on the idea of opening his own winery after taking a short viticulture course. In 1997, he and his wife bought 10 hectares (25 acres) and an adjacent block a year later. Montalto opened to the public in January 2002 as a family business that includes their daughter Heidi.

Montalto's rustic (for the Australian palate) "Pennon Hill" Grigio, fermented in stainless steel tanks, deliberately not oak, and, therefore, not as "mineral" as Italian-style, offers perfect accompaniment for pizza. Its grapes are picked early to retain their freshness, mineral backbone, and delicate fresh-fruit characteristics (apple and crisp nashi pear). By focusing on acid, rather than sugar, alcohol content is kept down, but aromatics are retained. Once de-stemmed and crushed, the grapes' resulting juice is chilled and settled in tanks before racked off and inoculated for fermentation at temperatures kept below 15 degrees Celsius (60 degrees Fahrenheit) to maintain fresh-fruit characters. The resulting wine is left on lees for a short time before racking, assembling, and bottling.

The winery's "Pennon Hill" Sparkling Cuvee is a bottle-fermented, traditional-method sparkling wine made from select parcels of Chardonnay, Pinot noir, and Pinot meunier, harvested in late February and early March. The base wine is fermented in stainless steel tanks. After settling time in-tank, it's bottled and triaged (sample drawn from the barrel for testing) in June. The wine is disgorged in batches as needed.

Also produced are Riesling, Chardonnay, Pinot Noir…and a Cuvee One that's 50% Chardonnay, 40% Pinot Noir, and 10% Pinot Meunier. There's Sauvignon Blanc/Semillon, Chardonnay, Rosé, Pinot Noir, Shiraz, a late-harvest Riesling, and a non-alcoholic Pinot Noir "Verj" that's like drinking juice straight from the press with bright fresh-berry fruit flavors balanced by a squeaky clean and crisp finish. The Pinot noir grapes used for the Verj are harvested early in the season, at around 60% of the ripeness at which the grapes are picked for table wine; this achieves a more bracing acidity that helps balance unfermented sugar. Following hand-harvesting, they're de-stemmed, crushed with skins still on (for the introduction of some color and delicate flavor), soaked for 3-4 hours, and, after pressing, cold-stabilized and sterile-filtered, before held in-tank at 2 degrees Celsius (35 degrees Fahrenheit), and, then, bottled.

The restaurant is in a modern wooden building with floor-to-ceiling glass windows overlooking the sculpture-dotted 20-hectare (50-acre) property. Awarded a coveted "Top Hat" in the *2010 The Age Good Food Guide*, and twice named the "Top Victorian Restaurant" by Winery, Restaurant and Catering Awards, the restaurant opens daily for lunch and, also, for dinner, on Fridays and Saturdays, year round, plus other evenings, depending upon the time of year. Under the guidance of chef, Barry Davis, the kitchen serves food inspired by regional France but anchored in the fresh seasonal regional produce of the Mornington Peninsula. Main courses can include: spatchcock, lamb, beef, veal, and duck.

There's a definite Italian atmosphere to the Cellar Door and Piazza, where rammed-earth walls, timber frames, and rough-hewn floorboards, make the most of nature. Even when the sun isn't shining, like the day we were there, misty rain on the grey timber exterior can match the grey leaves of nearby olive trees.

The open-air Garden Café offers casual, al-fresco dining on weekends and on public holidays, complete with long wooden tables and benches, and a menu of braised lamb shanks in winter, smoked salmon salad in summer, followed by estate-grown olives, home-made dips, and plates of temping cheese.

The experienced cellar door staff is passionate about wine, having worked in both vineyard and winery. In addition to its wine, it's a place to experience locally produced olive oil and other pantry products. Anyone who purchases a jar of the Strawberry Shiraz jam, like we did, is in for a treat.

During the Abundance Festival, lunch is available

in the Piazza accompanied by live entertainment. At which time, a special Cassoulet à la Catalan is available in the Marquee, in addition to the usual menu.

There's usually a game of bocce ball which visitors can play. Children can enjoy the petting zoo, have their faces painted, and/or take rides on the "Olive Express".

The main restaurant is also involved in the Festival, and, on Saturdays and Sundays, serves olive martinis and chilled wine to diners upon arrival, the dining room transformed into an olive grove as chef Barry Davis showcases Mediterranean flavors enhanced by estate-grown olive oil. There are even olive-pit spitting challenges with the winner awarded a championship crown!

CHAPTER TEN: THE PAST AND THE FUTURE
BALNARRING VINEYARD — QUEALY WINES

Cellar Door: Open every day 11:00 A.M. to 5:00 P.M.

Wines at the Cellar Door: Balnarring range: Pinot Grigio / Friulano, Chardonnay, Pinot Noir and late harvest Muscat. The Quealy range can be tasted at Merricks General Wine Store and includes a Pinot Grigio, Pinot Gris, many Pinot Noirs, Pobblebonk which Kathleen describes as her Pinot Grigio superblend and Rageous, a Sangiovese blend

Phone: +61 3 5983 2483

Website: www.quealy.com.au

Email: info@quealy.com.au

Directions: 62 Bittern-Dromana Road, Balnarring

At just about every winery we'd visited, at least one person told us we "had to" talk with Kathleen Quealy and Kevin McCarthy.

The vineyard, Balnarring, Kevin and Kathleen's pride and joy, is located on the lower northern slopes of Red Hill at the end of an unsealed drive leading from the gate to the cellar door and winery.

The "familiars" who greeted us, here, were two tan-colored kelpies; no other signs of life except the rooster quietly scratching the ground.

Neither a Taj Mahal, like Port Phillip Estate, nor a commercial restaurant-cum-winery, like Vines at Red Hill, Balnarring Vineyard is purely a working establishment. Once an apple store, it evolved into a winery. Its combination of old machinery with new technology is echoed by the common farm implements used as label graphics for its wines.

We poked our noses into the closest door. "Who the hell are you?" welcomed Kathleen who is described by Tim White, *Financial Review*, as the "Aussie Queen of Pinot Gris." By others, she's simply known as "the" Queen Bee.

She followed up our finally managed stammered introductions with a mischievous smile, and apologized for what might have seemed her initial gruffness. However, at the moment, she was genuinely too busy to talk, and waved a test tube in our direction by way of proof-positive. "Kevin is waiting for you in the house," she said, pointed in a general direction, and went back to whatever she was doing. We beat a hasty retreat.

Everybody (and I mean everybody) has a different word (crazy, insane, genius) to sum up Kathleen. Cheryl Lee, MPVA, thinks her "creative". What most immediately came to our minds were "eccentric"… "attractive"…"young".

Kevin said *he* definitely wouldn't call her crazy. He *would* call her creative and hard-to-keep-up-with. Once, she bought 600 fig trees; he (probably not even she) is now sure where she'd planted them all; the one most obvious, of course, is the glorious specimen standing watch at the winery's front door.

Kevin was recovering from a near-fatal run-in with a car. He'd been riding his bicycle along David Low Highway, near Noosa, Queensland, while up there for the Wine and Food Festival, but doesn't remember anything between glancing up to see the automobile only inches from his face and waking up in an ambulance. He'd ended up with broken ribs, and a punctured lung; lucky to be alive.

He ushered us into the kitchen and cleared a space at the table.

In 1980, Kevin studied Oenology at Roseworthy College, 50 kilometers (31 miles) north of Adelaide, on the road to the Clare Valley, just west of South Australia's famous Barossa Valley; the college was the only place in Australia, at the time, to study winemaking.

His fellow alumni, a tight-knit group who now comprise the top echelon of "Who's Who in Australia's Wine-Making", included Gordon Gebble, Murray Smith (one of the founders of the wine industry in the Orange district in New South Wales), Peter Douglas (now at Wynn's in the Coonawarra), and Eadie Price who established Amberley Estate Wines in Western Australia's Margaret River. Huon Hooke, well-known and respected wine writer and judge, was studying marketing at Roseworthy at the same time. All were eager to find out as much about wine-making as they could. Often, they learned as much from each other, on any given day, as they did from the available courses of study.

"In those days," Kevin said, "the only options were to go to places like Mildura and Sunraysia, which were, and still are, 'factory-style' wine-making areas best described as 'beyond marginal' for growing grapes."

As part of the course at Roseworthy, students were expected to gain practical on-the-job experience. As a result, Kevin worked South Australia's Barossa Valley, noted for its red wines resulted from vines planted by early European immigrants over 165 years before. Also, he clocked up experience north of Sydney in Hunter Valley, and in the Echuca area of Victoria at Tisdales. He ended up with an invaluable comprehension of wine differences in warmer versus cooler climes.

At the same time, Kathleen was at the Wagga Wagga campus of Charles Sturt University, studying viticulture.

After their meet up and marriage, the couple visited Elgee Park, situated at the end of Wallaces Road, Merricks North, owned at the time by Sarah and Baillieu (Bails) Myer, the latter the son of Sidney Myer, co-founder of Myer Emporium, Australia's largest chain of retail stores. Once Kathleen and Kevin saw the area already planted with Bordeaux and Riesling, they immediately thought it an ideal location for their own hoped-for vineyard.

Their son, Tommy, was born in 1988, as the couple became even more involved in the wine industry. Kevin started work at Elgee Park with Ian Hickinbotham who, like Kathleen, has been described as mad, crazy, and genius. Ian's father, Alan (Hick), initiated the first scientific wine-making course at Roseworthy College; Ian's son, Andrew, now runs Hickinbotham at Dromana.

As Kevin put it, "We were in the right place at the right time."

Kathleen joined us, cooked a fried egg, and, while still standing, began to eat it. She listened to our conversation, provided occasional interjections, and then headed back to complete whatever she was doing before her short respite.

By 1989, Kevin had helped establish Kings Creek Vineyard, with Andrew Hickinbotham. Over the next few years, he was involved with planting vines all over the Peninsula, including at Darling Park, in 1992, which provided the wine we had enjoyed with our recent meal at Vines of Red Hill.

Also, he helped at Seaforth Estate, the first vineyard we'd visited. All the while, Kathleen and he were two of only a select few, working in the area, who actually had had training in the field, making their input invaluable and always much in demand.

"Then, Kathleen had a bad car accident," Kevin said, "which tipped us into developing T'Gallant as a way of consolidating our life to cope with her recovery. It was strange how a serious accident precipitated our decision." There was yet another precipitous event when Kathleen suggested they plant Pinot gris grapes. It was an idea which Kevin, initially dismissed as unlikely to happen as no one was growing Pinot gris.

Kathleen, though, once she gets an idea into her head, won't be dissuaded, so Kevin rang a trusted friend, Janice McDonald, winemaker at Stella Bella in Western Australia's Margaret River; after Janice failed to dissuade Kathleen, Kevin talked to Australia's crème de la crème wine-makers and critics James Halliday and Huon Hooke who said it would be wiser to plant Pinot noir and Chardonnay, because "gris simply didn't have legs".

"There, you're trumped!" Kevin told Kathleen at the time. She merely smiled and said, "We're definitely doing it." As usual, she got her way, and the immediate problem became sourcing Pinot gris vines. In the end, they rang up Dr. Max Loder who was teaching at Charles Sturt University and had brought a Pinot gris clone with him from the Davis Campus of the University of California".

NOTE: While at Charles Sturt, in the 1970s, Max walked into a lecture room and introduced himself to thirty students of viticulture by asking, "Does anybody here want to make a good living from the wine business?" When a dozen hands shot up, he responded, "Good, leave now, and go straight through to the next classroom where the Wine Science students are.

Join them, for you will never be appreciated, nor paid appropriately for the work you do in the vineyard. Act now, or forever hold your peace!"

Even today, winemakers continue to make a great deal more money than those responsible for growing the grapes.

So, the resulting journey of the Australian variety of Pinot gris, the D1B7 clone, was from Alsace to the University of California to Charles Sturt University, via Max Loder, and, then, to Mornington Peninsula. Now, almost everyone there has vines that resulted from that original clone.

The late Mark Shield, wine journalist for *The Age* newspaper in Melbourne, wrote, in a short article about Kathleen's zeal for Pinot Gris: "The world, at the time, was in recession. No one was interested in developing the industry, certainly not the banks. The cuttings were sent to Rosebud nursery. An acre [.4 hectare] was planted at Darling Park, 2.5 acres [1 hectare] along Kentucky Road, and it all went from there. It wasn't all plain sailing. There were critics along the way."

Again, Kathleen joined us, this time sat down, and said part of the problem, even today, is that, "Australia still suffers from a cultural cringe towards the opinion of British wine critics, too many of whom only have good things to say about wines grown in regions they've vested interests in. Because none of these have Pinot gris, they're dismissive of the variety, ranking it lower than other premium varieties in the United Kingdom wine trade."

She insisted that Pinot Gris is a great variety, and the Mornington Peninsula is the best place to grow it. What's more, customers want to drink it, because it's good, not because winemakers suddenly want to grow it.

In 2004, Kathleen started making her own premium wines, under the Quealy brand, that advocate a "new style of wine", the results of Kathleen's many years of successful winemaking, concentrating on traditional Pinot Noir and Pinot Gris, but, also, to what Kathleen sees as their future. "The Alsace has been making blends forever," she said. "Blends are all about texture. Pinot Gris blends brilliantly with Pinot Noir. T'Gallant makes Holystone which is a blend of Pinot Noir and Chardonnay."

We found her 2008 Musk Creek Pinot Gris, like Kathleen, not a straightforward quaffing wine but one more complicated and better suited for sophisticated palates able to appreciate subtleties and complexities.

Kathleen makes the quaintly named Pobblebonk, styled after Italian "Super Whites", whose structure, style, and flavor results from clever variety combinations. Described by the winery as based on the warmth, raciness, tongue, and groove, of Pinot Grigio, it's combined with the textural dimension and gentle aromatics of Friulano. There's acidity and freshness from Chardonnay, with hints of aromatics from Muscat Giallo and Riesling. It's expressive, with great texture and lengthy palate, and adventurous in its style and flavor suited for cool climates.

Kathleen's Friulano, also called Tocai Friulano, or Sauvignonasse, is a variety native around the Adriatic Sea (Italy and Slovenia), and is revered for its natural acidity and gentle aromatics. The grape, an ideal blending partner for Pinot Grigio, thrives in maritime environments like Mornington.

Her Rageous is a blend of Sangiovese, Shiraz, and Pinot Noir.

Balnarring vineyard has some of the area's oldest premium Pinot noir (planted in 1982) and used exclusively in the production of Quealy Seventeen Rows Pinot Noir whose aroma is a mix of spice, tobacco and Chinese Plum, very open, very ripe, very rich, and with powerful taste. Kevin describes it as "in-the-style-of a Barolo". The grapes weren't used until 2007 when Kevin and Kathleen felt they were finally ready to produce a super-premium product.

Kathleen's second label, Balnarring Vineyard, offers modern but quirky wines at reasonable prices, with distribution limited to the Cellar Door, Merrick's General Wine Store in Red Hill, local venues, and in a very few restaurants in Melbourne. All of this label's wines are made from grapes grown on the vineyard.

The Style Spectrum—A Man with a Mission

In the early days, Kevin and Kathleen's winery leased a vineyard in Flinders on the Western Port side of the Peninsula that grew Chardonnay, Malbec, and Riesling Traminer. All that time, they were learning how to sell wine, run the business, and talk to the banks.

Their first vintage, 1992, was mainly sold to Hermann Schneider, at the time chef-owner of the legendary Two Faces restaurant in Melbourne.

In 1993, the couple had a good idea of what they would produce from their Pinot Gris. In 1994, they made their first "Tribute" (to Max Loder) wine, that mimicked those Alsace wines which had so blown their minds when they'd been in Europe.

In conjunction with the Australian Wine Research Institute (AWRI), they developed a Style Spectrum for Pinot gris (which they hope will eventually be known simply as a "Style Spectrum for Pinot G"). "There is enough debate about whether a wine should be called Pinot Gris, or Pinot Grigio," Kevin said. "The names mean nothing to anyone; they're simply the French and Italian words for the color of the grape. We needed to simplify things, take it all back to the basics."

Actually, it was in Alsace, as he tasted every French Pinot Gris wine he could get his hands on, discovering, to his amazement, some of them tasting exactly like Italian Pinot Grigio, that Kevin had his epiphany: a universal Style Spectrum was needed to distinguish "actual" differences. He spoke to Peter Godden, chair of the research group at the AWRI, which includes Australian marketers, winemakers, and independents, who embraced Kevin's challenge to calibrate Pinot-Gris using viable analysis.

"The scale that ranks a Riesling's sugar levels is

nothing compared to our rating of Pinot Gris," Kevin insisted. "We needed to identify style on a consistent basis. In the end, the AWRI analyzed the wine using a spectrophotometer which created a blueprint for each wine, much like a DNA fingerprint. We may not know what each of the 250,000 peaks represent on a graph, but enough are common between wines of similar taste to allow comparisons and ranking. This allowed us to take out the subjective and correlate the result to what people actually taste." He smiled as he added, "This is a world first." Even wine makers in Alsace and Italy are interested.

One of the most exciting aspects is that the whole range, or spectrum of styles, can be made just from accessing grapes grown in the Mornington Peninsula. Some ripen earlier than others, giving them widely different sugar content.

Jeni Port, *The Age* newspaper journalist, described the initiative, and she quoted winemakers in the region whose attitudes ranged from disinterest, because they made such small quantities for customers who already knew their wines, to qualified support from larger wineries whose labels included more than one Pinot G and style.

"Gris is a richer fuller-bodied wine made from riper grapes, and, often, with a touch of sweetness," Huon Hooke said. "Grigio…is lighter, crisper, drier, less complex, and is made from earlier harvested grapes, which naturally make lower alcohol wine…they are suited to different foods…imagine Pinot Grigio with oysters and the fuller softer white with stuffed and roasted chicken...it would make sense if gris and grigio had labels indicating their properties."

Hooke did, however, point out that, while the current tests recognized the different levels of alcohol, acids, sugars and phenolic compounds, mainly tannins, they were unable to account for residual sugars at a content higher than 10 grams per liter (1% w/v) which ruled out a lot of the Alsatian wines and even some from New Zealand.

Peter Godden, ARWI, noted that as wines age, they move up the scale of lusciousness, usually by about one point per year.

Sally Easton's online wine blog, *Wine Wisdom* (www.winewisdom.com), noted the launch of the Spectrum with agreement that, unlike other countries, where the styles are more regional, the position is confusing in Australia where "both pinot grigio and pinot gris are used interchangeably."

The Style Spectrum was provided along with the wines to judges at the 2010 Adelaide Wine Show; chairman of judges, Wynn's Coonawarra winemaker Sue Hodder, reported that the Spectrum helped both "psychologically and practically" as there is a tendency among some wine judges to have a negative bias towards certain varieties and styles. She sees the initiative as "a genuine attempt to find a way to help navigate consumers (and even winemakers) through a tricky situation, where the same grape variety is presented under two different names and across several styles, ultimately giving them the confidence to order a wine with a reasonable expectation of what it may smell, taste, and feel like."

The Spectrum presently goes from "crisp" (i.e. Grigio style) to "luscious" (Gris style). Later, the scale may be extended to take in dessert wines made from gris when affected by botrytis, or late-picked. Kevin and Kathleen only make a Pinot Gris dessert wine in a year the grapes are affected by Botrytis.

NOTE: In certain circumstances, usually requiring several wet spells, followed by dry, sunny conditions, a grey mold (*Botrytis cinerea*, or the famous Noble Rot) appears on the grapes and breaks down their skin, allowing water to evaporate, and so concentrates the sugars, and other solids, including acids and minerals. Because high concentrations of sugar inhibit the action of bacteria and yeasts, fermentation is inhibited, producing wines that may have as little as 6% alcohol. The resulting wine is ultra-sweet like the famous sweet dessert sauternes from Bordeaux.

Botrytised dessert wines are expensive, due to high cost and risk involved in production. Their volume is generally smaller than normal table wines. Also, many hours of hand tending are needed while the fruit remains on the vines an extra eight to ten weeks, constantly at risk from early frost, hail, and/or excessive rain; then, only the most-infected grapes are selected.

What continues to set Kathleen and Kevin apart from many winemakers is the love they've had for

Pinot Gris from the get-go, and how they've studied and researched the variety throughout the world. Many winemakers are dismissive of Pinot gris as a grape, simply because they haven't the confidence Kevin and Kathleen have in exploring its full potential.

A recent event that had Kathleen jumping up and down was the controversial removal of Pinot G (as it was specifically referred to) from the list of wines eligible for entry in the Australian Alternate Varieties Wine Show, because as the organizers noted: "Pinot G is no longer an alternative variety. There is no getting away from this fact. Over the last decade or so in Australia, Pinot G has experienced growth that other varieties could only dream about and currently makes up some 16% of our entries. In the 2009 vintage, it made up 2.4% of the total national crush, surpassed in premium whites only by Chardonnay, Sauvignon Blanc, and Semillon. There is now less Riesling crushed than Pinot G. Pinot G is also bigger than every red variety other than Shiraz, Cabernet, and Merlot. It's time to let Pinot G graduate, to take its place among the 'big boys'."

CHAPTER ELEVEN: THE ELEPHANT IN THE ROOM
T'GALLANT

Cellar Door: Open daily 10:00 A.M. to 5:00 P.M.

Restaurant: The Spuntino Bar is famous for its wood-fired Roman-style pizza. La Baracca embodies the chic rustica of a humming bistro. Open seven days a week for lunch and Thursday to Saturday for dinner

Wines at the Cellar Door: Juliet Pinot Grigio, Grace Pinot Grigio, Imogen Pinot Gris, Tribute Pinot Gris, Triumph Botrytis Pinot Gris, Chardonnay, Lot 2 Chardonnay, Viognier, Juliet Pinot Noir, Pinot Noir, Tribute Pinot Noir, Beechworth Sangiovese, Glenrowan Shiraz, Moscato

Phone: +61 3 5989 6565

Website: www.tgallant.com.au

Email: info@tgallant.com.au

Directions: 1385 Mornington-Flinders Road, Main Ridge 3928, on the corner of the Mornington-Flinders and Shands Roads

Some of the minor roads that crisscross the valleys of the Peninsula are still unpaved, hard-packed, and even flooded when local creeks run high. When we visited, these roads were dry, though, and in a good condition; we used them to short-cut to T'Gallant, the winery that Kevin and Kathleen sold to the Fosters Group corporation that owns some of the biggest names in Australian wines, including Lindeman's, Penfolds, Wolf Blass, and Wynn's Coonawarra Estate. Certainly, we'd taken a major step from those boutique wineries of our initial visits to a company genuinely into mass production. We were warned that T'Gallant grapes may come from regional vines, but its wines are no longer made locally; the grapes are now transported to South Australia for processing.

Given that four Pinot G wines are still offered by the winery proves how influential Kevin McCarthy remains as its winemaker.

By the way, "t'gallant" is a sailing term for the "top sail of a square-rigger sailing ship"; otherwise, it denotes "peak", "best", and "epitome". The Australian winery with that name boasts winemaking with expressive, natural, warm fermentations to ensure gossamer-like yeast aromas. Each wine is assessed regularly on its journey to the bottle, reductive characters blown off with air, and gentle fining, when required, using natural proteins found in isinglass and egg whites. Blends occur after fermentations.

The Cellar Master showed us the Juliet Pinot Grigio made from grapes grown in the Murray Darling, Strathbogie, and Riverina areas. Drought had affected some of these regions, and increased temperature had allowed the grapes to be harvested early, giving an alcohol content of 10.5%. The wine was designed to be a lower-priced light wine at the crisp end of the Pinot G Style Spectrum. It's recommended served with savory Italian-style food, or drunk on its own. Personally, we found it only "okay"; nothing to write home about.

T'Gallant's Grace scored 4.0 on the Style Spectrum, putting it up the Grigio/crisp end; it utilized grapes harvested from five vineyards, all with shallow pale-clay, or sandy soils, located on the coastal plain of the Mornington Peninsula. Cooler conditions than normal allowed for even and gentle ripening conditions—perfect for generating color and flavor, while retaining a balanced acidity. These had been blended with grapes from a T'Gallant east-west facing block. Wild yeasts kicked off fermentation and dryness, producing 12.5% alcohol. It's toted as "delightful when partnered with Asian-inspired dishes, such as Vietnamese cold rolls or Japanese sushi." We suggest drinking it within one to two years of release in order to best enjoy its zesty acidity and focused fruit flavor, having found it definitely a more finished wine than the Juliet we tasted before it.

The Imogen Pinot Gris was a combination of grapes from two local vineyards, juices perfect for out-right separate pressing with no fining; a wild ferment was allowed, with no yeast added, then blended. The finished wine, neither filtered nor fined, and made to drink immediately, had an alcohol level of 14.5%. We'd recommended it with roast quail (or the crispy skin of Vietnamese-pork belly), a side salad of parmesan cheese, and fresh pears. Definitely, we found it smoother, on the way down, than the Juliet or Grace.

The Tribute Pinot Gris was from fruit sourced from T'Gallant's West Block Vineyard and McCabe Vineyard. The latter is one of the oldest Pinot Gris blocks on the Peninsula. With its 14.5% alcohol, this late-harvest wine had a big taste that would likely go exceedingly well with bratwurst & Dijon mustard, caramelized onions, and traditional creamy mash; or, in summer, oven-roasted blue-eye fillet with a pesto crust topped with a tomato-onion-basil salsa.

Although we recommend these wines best drunk three to four years from vintage, the winery recently opened a fifteen-year-old Pinot G, stored under cork, which proved still good. So, if the wine has nice structure, it, likely, *can* be kept. Actually, there are some benefits to ageing. While the wine may lose some of its vibrancy and freshness and even get a deeper color, there does tend to be a leveling out of peaks and troughs.

NOTE: It's all ideally stored at 10 degrees Celsius (50 degrees Fahrenheit), by the way, *not* at refrigerator temperature.

Smaller boutique wineries often allow a couple of years in the bottle.

T'Gallant sometimes makes a fifth Pinot G version. This is its dessert wine, made from botrytis-affected Pinot gris.

For those drinkers not "into" Pinot G, T'Gallant offers its Claudius Mornington Peninsula white wine, inspired by the wines of Josko Gravner in Friuli (in far North Eastern Italy, near the Slovenia border). A blend of Chardonnay (80%), Moscato Giallo (5%) and Gewurztraminer (15%), it's made using red wine techniques such as extended maturation on skins, 100% new oak, and bottling without fining or cold settling.

Wine no longer made on the premises, the main buildings have been converted into La Baracca Trattoria and The Spuntino Bar. The former, with its distinct rustic feel, is surrounded by a fig grove planted by Italian pioneers in the 1930s, and by a garden that includes artichokes, herbs, seasonal flowers, and features an Italian farmhouse menu using seasonal produce. The latter allows visitors to unwind to music (live on weekends), in the shade of fig trees, or within the sheltered warmth afforded from wood-fire ovens that serve up Italian-inspired food, like crispy pizza, accompanied by the winery's Pinot Grigio.

Group bookings for dinners, and other functions, can be arranged.

NOTE: Each year, T'Gallant holds a Tre Gusti Mushroom Forage. Over a series of weekends, in May, participants forage in the vineyard for saffron milk caps and slippery jacks. Afterwards, they partake in a cooking demonstration with food stylist Louise Lechte. In 2010, the cucina menu featured warm mushroom cappuccino, mushroom paté on crostini, forestière mushroom pasta with mascarpone and pine nuts, as well as freshly char-grilled wild mushroom pizza with lashings of taleggio.

Cooking classes, in two-hour sessions, are held in the barrel garden and cucina during the year, and utilize seasonal produce from the garden.

Some locals are wary of T'Gallant's transition from boutique winery to its current position under the behemoth Foster's Group umbrella. The obvious respect their peers still seem to have for former owners, Kevin and Kathleen, as regards the knowledge of and zeal for wine that the couple brought to the area, didn't prevent community arguments against T-Gallant's development application for extended licensing hours and a larger restaurant, citing that T'Gallant wines are no longer made on-site, or even sourced from locally grown product.

In February, 2010, the Victorian Civil and Administrative Tribunal rejected Foster's application for expansion.

CHAPTER TWELVE: WINING AND FINE DINING
RED HILL ESTATE

Cellar Door: Open daily 11:00 A.M. to 5:00 P.M. except Christmas Day

Restaurant: Max's at Red Hill Estate—a la carte dining 7 days, seats 100 people. Lunch 7 days from noon Dinner Friday & Saturday from 7pm.

Wines at Cellar Door: Reserve Label Chardonnay and Pinot Noir, Red Hill Estate label sourced from different vineyards in the area: Blanc de blanc and Blanc de noir–sparkling wines made on Chardonnay and a Pinot Noir / Pinot Meunier blend respectively, Pinot Grigio, Sauvignon Blanc, Chardonnay, Rosé, Pinot Noir, Shiraz

Bookings can be made for tutored wine tastings, plus personal wine tastings, for corporate functions and events in and around Melbourne

Phone: +61 3 5989 2838

Website: www.redhillestate.com.au

Email: info@redhillestate.com.au

Accommodations—Max's Retreat and Max's Retreat at Red Hill Estate: 9 Station Road, Red Hill South luxury accommodation with four large bedrooms with en-suite and deck, oversized living/dining room, fully equipped kitchen, beautiful manicured outdoor areas, close to Red Hill attractions; Max's Retreat Vineyard Cottage, recently renovated, with two bedrooms with en-suite, one with a corner spa, two sitting rooms and an open-plan kitchenette, dining room, and a large outdoor deck

Directions: 53 Shoreham Road, Red Hill South

In, around, and on Red Hill, where wild bullocks once roamed, and where kangaroos used to be counted in the scores, there are still those who refer to the place by its old name—Bald Hill.

As early as 1862, John Arkwell purchased land here and planted an orchard of mixed fruit trees and blackberries. In the 1870's, H. B. Simon, known in his day as "Simon the Frenchman", grew grapes to make his own wine.

Later, James Wiseman, a Scottish blacksmith, set up home and shop.

Red Hill Coolstores, providing warehousing for local produce, opened in 1920, and still stands today. Eventually, a railway line appeared between Red Hill and Bittern, allowing local farmers to take their produce to Melbourne.

While the area progressed into a successful farm, cattle-ranch, and horse-breeding community, grape-growing, surprisingly, wasn't nearly as successful.

Vine diseases in the cool climate, and well as infestations of phylloxera, saw many growers abandoning their attempts at commercial vineyards.

Only in 1973, with the advent of modern technology to cope with managing vini-cultivation in the area, did the Ballieu-Myer family establish the Elgee Park vineyard and winery, followed by Main Ridge Estate.

In 1979, Sir Peter and Lady Derham purchased 8 hectares (20 acres) for cattle grazing and another 12 hectares (30 acres) for a 1989 transformation into a vineyard for various varietals grapes. Their Red Hills Estate winery was outfitted with state-of-the-art equipment, and Jenny Bright was brought in as its first full-time vintner.

Red Hill's second label "Waterholes Creek", named after the creek on the property that feeds a wetlands area, was launched in 1993.

In 2000, Bentco Pty Ltd bought into Red Hill Estate.

In 2006, Red Hill Estate merged with the historic Hunter Valley producer Arrowfield Estate and began trading under the collective name "The InWine Group Australia" which produces a full range of wines, from high-quality premium labels to volume-driven products, using contract growers where appropriate. Brenton Martin, CEO, says, "There are great synergies between the two wineries which will allow us to make better wines more efficiently, making us more competitive at all price points".

Upon our arrival, we were greeted by Garth Noonan at the cellar door, and he soon had us with a glass in-hand of the only Pinot the winery has made for the last six years. Although called Pinot Grigio by the winery, most customers refer to it as Pinot Gris. It's a sub-regional blend of fruit from Tuerong, Merricks North, and Red Hill. Handpicked fruit is de-stemmed, chilled, and pressed. A portion of the ferment occurs in old French barriques, the other in stainless tanks. Upon completion of primary fermentation, wine is allowed to settle and remains on lees for about six months until the wine is transferred out of barrel for bottling. The alcohol level usually averages around 13%; the bouquet and palates are delicate and restrained with hints of pear, apple, musk and blossom. It's best drunk young.

Red Hill Estate wines are sold through Liquorland, and by Dan Murphy (Australia's largest wine retailers). They're widely available in restaurants and are distributed internationally to Japan, Denmark, USA, Canada, Sweden, Singapore, Poland, and Hong Kong.

The Red Hill Estate Cellar Door retains a traditional winery atmosphere with its smell of oak thick in the air. It features a range of printed information to guide novices through the secrets of winemaking, as well as educational displays from budburst to bottle.

There's an old wine barrel artistically rendered into the likeness of one of those deep-sea fish that seems all teeth; a lighted lure accompanies, made from a couple of corks on the end of rusty clippers. My immediate thought was that the piece should be entered into the Montalto sculpture competition.

The home vineyard consists of 10 hectares (24

acres) of predominantly Pinot noir and Chardonnay. In addition, a number of vineyards are leased from a number of Mornington Peninsula growers. Long-time contracts allow for close relationships between winery and growers.

The largest managed vineyards are in Vineyard Lane, Tuerong, in the warmer northern part of the peninsula. It has mostly gentle north-facing slopes and has proved an excellent and consistent source of quality fruit. The winery's well-known Mornington Peninsula Cabernet Sauvignon comes from a small protected north-facing 2-hectare (5-acre) vineyard, the Briars, at Mt Martha.

Pinot gris is grown, without irrigation, alongside Pinot noir, Chardonnay, and Pinot meunier, on the 9 hectares (22 acres) of the Red Hill Estate.

More Pinot gris is grown on the 20-hectare (50-acre) Range Road Vineyard in Moorooduc at the northerly base of Red Hill. Chardonnay, Pinot noir, and a variety of French clones, are, also, grown there.

There's Pinot gris, Pinot noir, and Sauvignon blanc grown in the 6-hectare (16-acre) Tuerong Junction Vineyard just over the fence from Range Road.

Two-hectare (5-acre) Kentucky Gate consistently produces some of the winery's best Chardonnay and Pinot fruit. Something about this particular patch provides grapes with flavors very focused and intense.

Just out of the hills, to the north, is 9-hectare (22-acre) Marinda Park that produces, from its mature vines, Pinot noir, Pinot gris, and Chardonnay, all of exceptional body.

Finally, on the south side of Red Hill, is the 19-hectare (46-acre) Merricks Grove Vineyard that produces Pinot noir, Chardonnay, Pinot gris, and Sauvignon blanc.

Given the large amount of Pinot gris under cultivation, at different latitudes, elevations, aspects, and in varying soil types, on these six parcels of land, we were initially surprised to discover only the one Red Hill Estate Pinot G. However, it's probably because of this winery's ability to draw its fruit from several vineyards that ensures the uniqueness of its one wine, as well as ensures consistent quality of the wine which is widely distributed through major outlets.

The philosophy of Red Hill Estate is that its wine should taste of place, and be true to variety, vineyard, region, and vintage; winemaking focused on honoring the sum of those parts.

Luke Curry, with a Bachelor of Science (Biological) from Latrobe University, began working at Red Hill Estate in the vineyard in 1999. In 2000, with a holistic view of the wine industry, he gained experience in sales and marketing, and then commenced a Bachelor of Applied Science (Wine Science) at Charles Sturt University, followed by seven years of experience at premium cool-climate facilities in the Yarra Valley and Mornington Peninsula. In 2007, he became Red Hill Estate's Senior Wine Maker, determined to make wines that explore the relationship between vineyard site, viticultural practices, and winemaking.

The winery has, since, more than once been named "Victorian Vineyard of the Year", plus receiving the

"National Tourism Award for the Best Winery". It has scored over 260 medals in show arenas, including trophies for its Classic Release Chardonnay, Classic Release Pinot Noir, Red Hill Estate Chardonnay, Red Hill Estate Shiraz, Red Hill Estate Blanc de Noirs, and Red Hill Estate Blanc de Blanc. It has received recognition for its ultra-modern approach to pest and disease management; vineyard manager, Tyson Lewis, head of the technical committee for the Mornington Peninsula Vignerons Association, has been singled out for recognition because of his efforts in following an environmentally friendly approach to viticulture.

Besides its wine, its Cellar Door offers a wide range of local produce: delicious chocolate sauce from Red Hill Mud; sensational cherry jam, plum jam, and quince paste jams from nearby Ellisfield Farm; and some of the best olives and olive oil from one of the oldest olive groves, La Campagna, on the Peninsula.

Red Hill Estate and Max's Restaurant overlook magnificent panoramic vistas of rolling hills, trees, Western Port and Phillip Island; all of which Ian Sutton, former President of the Australian Winemakers Federation, once described as the "best views of any vineyard in the world".

The restaurant, which has won numerous awards, most recently "Australia's Favourite Modern Australian" in the Lifestyle Food Channel's I Love Food Awards, and "Tourism Restaurant of the Year" in the 2010 Victorian Tourism Awards, serves internationally-inspired cuisine prepared by Max Paganoni and carefully matched with Red Hill Estate wines. It was opened to the public in 1993 with light snacks and accompanying wine tastings which proved so popular that a hundred-seat extension, and the more comprehensive menu, were added.

There are plans for major future expansion that not only include a new Cellar Door and restaurant entrance, glassed-in fronts to open them to even more spectacular views over Western Port, but a doubling of the restaurant size, with a café-style patio looking out toward the sea. Also, self-contained on-site accommodations with conference facilities have been proposed.

It will be interesting to see if this development suffers the same degree of opposition, and consequences, the T'Gallant's efforts did. Perhaps, the fact that the majority of Red Hills Estate wines are still grown from local grapes may work in its favor.

CHAPTER THIRTEEN: TRUE PINOTPHILES
RAHONA VALLEY VINEYARD

Open by appointment only
Wines available: Pinot Noir, Pinot Meunier, Pinot Gris, Pinot Rosé and Sparkling "Blanc de Noirs". Priority allocations given to members on mailing list
Phone: +61 3 5989 2924
Website: www.rahonavalley.com.au
Email: pinot@rahonavalley.com.au
Directions: 6 Ocean View Avenue, Red Hill South 3937

Having visited the area's largest and oldest wineries, we next visited one of its smallest. Rahona's owners, John and Leonie Salmons, while very interested in our search for the perfect Mornington Peninsula Pinot G, warned that their vineyard, 2 hectares (4 acres) in total, has only two rows of Pinot gris: enough for just one barrel, most years. "We haven't even had the gris long," John added, "this is only our third vintage. We've put most of it into a new French oak barrel to see what will happen."

Local planning regulations prevent Rahona from being a traditional Cellar Door. John and Leonie aren't allowed to have people come and sample, or buy, their wines, only "inspect" the vineyard. "Not walk through it, though," John insisted, echoing Nat White's fear of visitors spreading disease via the soles of their shoes.

Only John was at home the day we visited, and we sat chatting on the landing of Rahona's small wine-making and storage area, surveying its neat vineyard lay-out, and sharing a bottle of its surprisingly excellent lone Pinot Gris.

"George," John said, seeming to pull the name out of his hat, "also has had problems with complaints about visitors. He's not allowed to have buses, and, once, his son's architecture class arrived in a school bus on a non-winery visit, and the council officer arrived a little while later."

"George who?"

"Why, George Mihaly, of Paradigm Hill, of course. You *are* going to see him, aren't you?"

We checked the wineries remaining on our list. Paradigm Hill wasn't there.

"If you're interested in Pinot Gris, you simply must talk to him," John assured. "He's a legend. Each year, he launches his new season's vintage during the Melbourne Cup [a famous horse race that pretty much "stops the nation"], and sells out of all his Pinot Gris before the weekend is over. In my opinion, his is the best I've ever come across."

In the 1980's, John and Leonie became interested

in wine, and they toured the cellar doors, learning as much as they could. In 1990, they purchased a small block at the end of Ocean View Avenue. At first, they just sold grapes to other growers, but, in 2000, when John retired from his day job as an accountant, Leonie, decided he needed something to keep him busy. "Making wine is an indulgence for me," he said. "I could have taken up golf, but how many days a week does that occupy?"

We got the distinct impression that Leonie would have found John's energy difficult to deal with on any off-day. With a wry grin, John admitted that, like many of his peers, he could have bought a boat, but, then, he'd never have seen a return on his investment. This way, he does get a bit of money back "every now and then." Besides, the winery is something in which the couple can jointly be involved, Leonie contributing in all aspects of the vineyard.

"You might say I needed another challenge, and I haven't quite conquered the art of making white wine, yet," he said. Judging from the sample we were drinking, though, we begged to differ. He attributes his success largely to Leonie's palate which he describes as "much better" than his. "She's 'non-stop' in coming up with ideas and was the driving force behind our getting involved in sparkling wines," he said. "We make a Pinot Rosé, using D5V12 Pinot Noir (the champagne clone)." Again, in indication of his background in accounting, he added, "Trying to make just pure Pinot Noir wouldn't be a good return on my money.

Mind you, real Pinot consumers would scoff at rosé, but it's very punter-friendly and will still be good in two or three years."

A few years ago, at Leonie's suggestion, they grafted two rows over to Pinot gris which is harvested in late March to early April. They started making the wine four years ago, but only produce twenty to thirty boxes a year.

"Did you know that in London, Pinot Gris is the most ordered luncheon wine in restaurants?" he asked. "They're looking for something light which won't compete with salads."

He estimates Leonie and he have 5,000 vines in total, all tended by hand. John doesn't use battery-powered shears, although, he said, mischievously, "I believe micro-surgeons are quite happy with them for making such clean cuts, allowing fingers to be easily sewn back on." Instead, he uses hand shears and employs contract labor to pull the vines.

They harvest some of the grapes in mid March to ensure the high acid and low sugar perfect for their sparkling wines. Also, this helps to thin out the vines and allow further ripening of those Pinot grapes remaining.

A few winemakers bottle immediately before harvest, so the barrels don't dry out, but John finds it all too hectic at that time of the year.

Some vintners just see Pinot Noir as a "good summer red", not as heavy as a Shiraz or Cabernet (which John describes as "entry level wines"). John said, "Good

Pinot Noir can have much more depth, elegance and complexity than those two wines. It has got good acid and fruit." He likes the earthy, forest floor flavors that are so often associated with fine Pinot Noir.

Like most winemakers, John uses sulfur dioxide to stabilize the wine to prevent oxidation and acetic acid development. Sometimes, he uses microscopic amounts of copper to remove any hydrogen sulphide (bad egg smell) taint that can arise if the yeast runs out of free nitrogen in the juice and starts to digest proteins.

NOTE: Sulfur dioxide can be added as either the free gas, as it is in large wineries, or as potassium meta bisulphate which disassociates in the wine to release sulfur dioxide. This is why many wine labels state that the wine may contain sulfites.

As for copper, in the olden days, winemakers would drop a penny in the barrel, and it would go quite black with a copper sulphide coating, but, nowadays, copper sulfate crystals are used. They dissolve easily, and the amount of copper added can be measured in thousandths of a gram.

The practice of adding sulfur to wines began in Roman times. Even wine-makers who pride themselves on using purely organic methods use it.

The fermentation process stops by itself when all the sugar is consumed, and the sulfur dioxide is then added to prevent spoilage. Yeast is, in fact, very tolerant of sulfur dioxide, whereas acetic-acid-producing bacteria are very sensitive to it.

John is very proud of their sparkling wine, "Pink Fizz", made from Pinot noir. The grapes are crushed immediately after picking, the juices taken away from the skins and fermented dry, sugar and yeast added at bottling. Crud forms at the bottom, but, after a year, this is disgorged so all the yeast dies. The bottles are topped off with a liqueur of wine and sugar. Fifty milliliters (about 10 teaspoons) of the latest Pinot noir are added at the end. A "White Fizz" is also produced.

Rahona Valley Vineyard also produces "Bob's Cider", in honor of Leonie and John's dog, Bob, who John described as "owning them jointly". The dog made his presence known, with much tail-wagging, and sniffing, at our ankles.

"Are you aware," John asked, his voice showing disgust, "that some cider makers use reconstituted apples while others just use maize? These are fermented, and when the alcohol is stabilized, a bucketful of apple juice is added and marketed as cider. Not good enough for Bob." The dog lifted his head in ready agreement. "To make the Rahona Vineyard's cider, I buy two barrels of apple juice and ferment it in the barrel."

Their wine and cider retail through a wide range of Melbourne cellars and Canberra retailers in addition to subscribers to their mailing list.

While a few places we visited mentioned heat, cold weather can, also, cause problems for wine makers. Rahona Valley Vineyard is lucky in that it only gets the occasional light frost in winter, and, so far, never in spring when serious damage can be done.

NOTE: Primordial cells that are involved in the formation of the next-year's grapes differentiate in late spring and early summer on current year's canes. If there are no developed canes, at the time, because the new shoots have been "burnt off" by frost, or by multiple frosts, there aren't any embryonic bud cells remaining to provide next year's harvest.

For shoots to be negatively affected, they must be chilled to -2° Celsius (28 degrees Fahrenheit) or less. If there's lots of dew, the effect can be mitigated by the formation of ice crystals on the shoots which actually limit cooling. This is why severe frost events are often associated with droughts when the atmosphere is too dry for ice crystals to form.

Commonly, vineyards in frost-prone areas have defensive measures, such as windmills, helicopters, water sprays, or "frost pots" (cans filled with sump oil and other wastes that are burnt to provide a smoke blanket that prevents heat loss by radiation).

"There are a few Peninsula vineyards that have had problems with frost, but not recently—as far as I know," John said. "We have had problems some years with cool spring weather that leads to a poor fruit set." In the 2001/2002 season, it was serious, and the crop was virtually wiped out. It happened again in 2006/2007, on a lesser scale, just enough to ensure that fruit loads were perfect for Pinot Noir, because there was no over cropping.

John and Leonie regard themselves as true Pinotphiles. Leonie has even written a lyrical exposition on the Pinot noir grape, based on material from well-known wine writers such as Jancis Robinson, Hugh Johnson, Remington Norman, Kermit Lynch and Matt Kramer:

"To pinotphiles, be they growers, winemakers, or imbibers, finding the perfect Pinot has a similar status as the search for the Holy Grail. Each year there's that sense of excitement. What will this season bring?

"Serious Pinot lovers feel that the sensory experience of a good Pinot can elevate one to another level analogous in music, literature or art, say, as Musak is to Mozart, Pot Boiler to Proust, or Graffiti to Giotto!

"The Pinot noir vine is variously described as capricious, fickle, sulky, or moody. In other words, it's hard to grow. To mention a couple of its demands, it doesn't like wind, or an extreme of heat and cold at fruit set, and insists on a long warm ripening period.

"The wine can be colorless and acidic if the fruit is not ripe, or flavorless and jammy if ripened too early. This is bad Pinot. At its best, however, when there is optimum ripeness in terms of flavor, sugar, and acid, it is considered sublime, and the superlatives flow: magnificent perfume, silky opulence, elegant, even sensuous. In addition, after a period of bottle ageing, Pinot will develop a spectrum of secondary flavors much sought after by enthusiasts and commonly described as savory or 'forest floor'.

"Pinot is described as having the greatest propensity

of all grapes to reflect the 'terroir' (site, soil, climate, sunlight) in which it is grown. Indeed, it is mentioned that monks in medieval times chose Pinot noir as the one grape variety that most eloquently reflected the voice of God through the land. Thus, unlike other grape varieties, such as Cabernet sauvignon and Shiraz, Pinot can taste different in different locations, even as close as across the road! And given the conditions mentioned, each vintage will always be different from the last. One can liken this to a great work of art: Each is a one-of and can't be duplicated or made to a formula.

"Pinot is a natural accompaniment of food. It's great with its traditional Burgundian partners of poultry and game, but, also, good with deep-sea fish, risottos, and lightly-flavored Asian dishes.

"Burgundy is the home of the great Pinots, and from where pinotphiles gain inspiration and a certain amount of aspiration. Of course, we can't emulate the Burgundies completely, because we're not in Burgundy, are we? Pinots from outside Burgundy will always be different, because they reflect their own particular 'terroir'.

"In the cool climate areas of Australia, and particularly at Rahona Valley, on the Mornington Peninsula, in Victoria, we incorporate the components of north-facing site to allow maximum exposure to the sun, well-drained ancient basalt soil, and an open canopy, to deliver beautiful disease-free ripe fruit. Minimal wine making techniques, and a restrained use of new oak, allow this fruit to develop into an elegant wine, with complex fruit flavors, and well-balanced tannin and acidity. As the Burgundians say, 'It's all in the fruit. The wine makes itself'.

"So, there we have it. Pinot is like an elusive siren, to challenge, and try us, but always, hopefully, to beguile us."

CHAPTER FOURTEEN: THE LEGEND
DR. GEORGE MIHALY— PARADIGM HILL

Cellar Door: Open on the first weekend of the month only. Please book groups greater than six
Cellar Door Winery Sales: 100% estate-grown and crafted Pinot Noir, Shiraz, Rosé, Riesling and Pinot Gris
Phone: +61 3 5989 9000
Website: www.paradigmhill.com.au
Email: info@paradigmhill.com.au
Directions: 26 Merricks Road Merricks Vic 3916

One thing noticed on our drive from Sydney, the wineries in the Yarra Valley, judging by their names, are owned by people mainly of Italian descent. Possibly that, and the hotter, drier climate of the area, explain why the area's Pinot Gs are more like the Italian Pinot Grigios. In the cool environment atop Red Hill, growers are more inclined to the French influence, and their wines reflect that.

At Paradigm Hill, golden retriever, Jemima, met

us. She's the official "Vineyard Security Officer", "Cellar Door Welcome Manager", "Pre-adolescent Entertainment", and "Cellar Door Visitor Alert Coordinator".

NOTE: *WINE DOGS OF AUSTRALIA*, now in its second edition, consisting of 300 pages of gorgeous photos taken by Craig McGill and Sue Elliott, mentions "Jemima of Paradigm Hill" as having an obsession with socks, even known to steal them from visitors.

We stopped at Paradigm Hill, because John Salmons, at Rahona Valley Vineyards, insisted George Mihaly was a must-meet. Luckily, George hadn't yet left for Alsace, France, where he was headed for talks with French winemakers. He tries to go at least every other year to keep up with what's going on within the European wine-making community.

Paradigm Hill sells seventy percent of its product through restaurants, and ninety-five percent of those have at least one "Chef's Hat"—*The Age* newspaper's restaurant ranking. We had only been talking for a very few minutes when George took an incoming call from John Clancy—sommelier at Guillaume Bennelong, the restaurant at the Sydney Opera House, who needed some Paradigm Hill Pinot Noir.

Although George's wines sell out quickly each year, and are always in great demand, he has no plans for expansion. He has 20 hectares (50 acres) of land, only part of which are planted with vines. "I worked out that if I plant any more, I'd need to employ another worker,"

George said, "and the wage needed to cover that would be taken by the one extra hectare (three extra acres), so it's pointless. In any case—what we have is more than enough for Ruth and I to manage!"

The extreme popularity of his Pinot Gris meant there was none left from previous vintages for us to taste. Before George poured Pinot Noir, by way of substitute, he went for accompanying snacks. He's a strong believer that wine should *always* be served with food. It's nothing to do with sensible consumption of alcohol, purely with taste. He disagrees with the usual practices of cellar doors to sell wines by their lonesome. Since Paradigm doesn't have tastings every day, only once a month, each time they do, George's wife, Ruth, formerly a chef, carefully selects food to complement whatever wines are available for tasting. Actually, her role at the winery is far more than *just* that. "As a viticulturist, she oversees the vines," George said. "I just make the wine." He sees himself as caretaker of his grapes, just doing his best to make sure nothing goes wrong; his wife, Ruth, is the true genius in the vineyard who turns the grapes into wine.

In the late 1990's, after retirement from a career in medical research and pharmaceuticals, George entered wine-making, under the tutelage of Nat White of Main Ridge. "You couldn't hope to meet a more generous, gentle person," George said of his mentor. "Nat brought the winemakers of the area together as a community."

When it came time for George's initial planting, he decided it would be two reds and two whites. While he agreed with Nat White that Mornington Peninsula was perfect for Pinot noir and Chardonnay, he ended up following Kevin and Kathleen's initiative to plant Pinot gris and was confident that Riesling would, also, do well. George, Kevin, and Kathleen agree that the Mornington Peninsula is perfectly suited to Pinot gris. "Because of this, we (all the wine growers) can bask in the pleasures of each other's glories." In fact, the wineries of the area have taken the Alsace method so far that the winemakers George regularly meets in France are often amazed by the amount of expertise George "brings to the table" and is happy to share with his buyers via informative wine labels.

In the end, he grafted all his stock onto disease-resistant rootstock. It was a risk-management choice that cost him six dollars a pot, instead of 80 cents, but it avoided the devastatingly humungous expensive, not to mention the down time that would result, anywhere from three to ten years, if and when Phylloxera hit susceptible vines. Despite that initial precaution, he still follows anti-phylloxera protocols that insist visitors be kept from traipsing through his vines.

He echoed agreement with many to whom we'd spoken who truly believe each area has its own natural characteristics suited for specific varieties of grape. "Even within the Mornington Peninsula, there are differences between grapes grown in the lower altitude areas of Moorooduc and Dromana, and those grown up on Red Hill," he offers as proof. "The ambient temperature, rainfall, nature of the clay subsoil, degree of water retention, amount of irrigation…all these… affect how deep in the soil the roots go to impart a different flavor to the wine."

The Peninsula picks up prevailing west-to-east rain bands which have become more and more prevalent. Area dams and tanks were full when we were there, moss actually growing on the surfaces of car parks.

Paradigm's grafted Riesling is a cool varietal that ripens later on the Peninsula than if planted elsewhere. So, with low phenolic development, it closely resembles the Rieslings of Alsace.

Paradigm's Pinot gris is cropped for between 1.5 to two tons per .4 hectare (1 acre). George believes one of the main reasons for a drop in quality, elsewhere, is fruit is so often cropped for eight tons per .4 hectare (1 acre)—which he doesn't agree with. "Growers should thin the vines, and at Paradigm Hill we do, with the aim of getting all the fruit to develop at the same time by removing any fruit that is either lagging behind or racing ahead in its development."

To this end, he now adopts vertical-shoot positioning (VSP) canopy training where shoots are constrained to grow into canes between several pairs of wires that are affixed to either side of trellis posts along wires.

He cane prunes his Pinot noir and Pinot gris; he spur prunes the rest of his vineyard where the Shiraz and Riesling grow.

He follows the Big Vine Theory (BVT) which is low-density planting, ensuring the root-ball of each vine establishes itself in a way that seems to help to balance the vine and constrain the vigor of the plant.

"Temperature is crucial," he said, echoing what we'd heard at Ten Minutes by Tractor.

In 2009, at the ripening point when Pinot gris skins turn mauve, and Pinot noir goes black (veraison), the Mornington Peninsula had 80-kilometers-per-hour (50-miles-per-hour) winds from the northwest, directly incoming from central Australian deserts, generating lots of heat. This was just a week before disastrous fires occurred north of Melbourne. As a result, seventy percent of the Paradigm crop was lost. Most of the other wineries in the area were similarly affected. Photos of grape clusters from the same vine but on different sides of George's canopy trellises show fruit of one side shriveled like raisins, the fruit of the other side still plump and black. After a great deal of "manicuring" of the vines, and removal of any damaged bunches, only the good fruit was harvested.

"Where normally we'd get 150 to 200 cases, that year we only got 60 cases of Pinot gris," he said. Paradigm had to limit restaurants to a total of six bottles of wine, even more severe rationing than in normal years when the wine is naturally in short supply.

George and Ruth don't pick until the acid and the sugar levels are right (not just sugar level). "Obviously, you also have to ensure the grape is physiologically ripe, as well as bio-chemically ripe. Look at the pips; taste them; they should have a crunchy taste, the skins should be friable. Look at the tannins. It's hard to make good wine without the ability to approach it with wine sensibility and science."

NOTE: The juice pressed from grapes becomes wine when the sugars present are consumed by yeasts and converted to alcohol (ethanol) as a by-product in a process known as *fermentation*. The sugar levels increase as the grape ages on the vine and dry out.

In the presence of excess oxygen, ethanol becomes oxidized back to acetaldehyde. This is what creates the acrid, sherry like character of some wines. To prevent this, the wine maker has to minimize the exposure of finished wines to air. Because of their higher phenolic content, reds are less susceptible to acetaldehyde production than are whites.

George took us into the building he calls "The Cave", where the majority of his wine is stored, and he promised us a sampling of his Pinots gris currently maturing in French oak casks for six months to facilitate texture, rather than the character of the fruit. There are "three" skins of insulation to The Cave, providing temperature and humidity control. The day we were there it was 15 degrees Celsius (65 degrees Fahrenheit) inside and about 28 degrees Celsius (over 80 degrees Fahrenheit) outside. He uses Taransaud barrels. "These don't come cheap, $1,750 for each new barrel. Though, thanks to exchange rates, I was able to get them for $1,250-$1,300, this last time. The cooper is fanatical about the quality of his product, so I trust him implicitly. The wood is from the Vosges forest, so the oaky flavor isn't strong, allowing savory, earthy characters to shine through, and supporting the natural spice of the Pinot gris variety."

While we were there, he added a small amount of the wine stored in nearby stainless steel tanks for the express purpose of "topping off" the barrels, noting that each fortnight 600 milliliters (just under 1 pint) of the barreled wine can be lost through evaporation. Topping off reduces exposure of the remaining wine to air and thus unwanted oxidation.

As well as allowing us to sample some of this next batch of Pinot Gris, he also removed a sample of Pinot Noir (exceptionally clear and tasty, despite several more months of needed maturation) from a barrel of Pinot Noir that had been harvested from one tiny section of the vineyard that produces wine fragrantly perfumed, because of the soil. Originally, this parcel of wine used to be blended with the other Pinot Noir wines, but, now, it's treated separately by George, producing only one or two barrels (25 to 50 cases), that he calls "Les Cinq" because of the sole five rows of vines from which it's grown.

The rest of his Pinot Noir is L'amisage (the wise friend). George makes it from the crush and blend of two different clones. It has a more masculine tannin structure, more-in-your-face voluptuousness, more brutish and brooding, than Les Cinq which is decidedly feminine. The two wines, though, are good examples of how terroir can be expressed.

NOTE: George also uses a small number of barrels from the French cooperages St Martin and Gillet for his Pinot Noir and would usually use more Gillet barrels for Shiraz, feeling them better suited to bigger-flavored wines.

Nothing is added to the grape juice, and it is allowed to ferment slowly at 10-to-12 degrees Celsius (50-54 degrees Fahrenheit). George believes warmer fermenting cooks off the pretty floral character of the variety. Silently, we wondered what he'd think of the barrels we'd seen sitting in the sun in front of Underground Winemakers' cellar door.

He admitted it's easier to control the fermentation process in stainless steel tanks, and how it takes a different view of things to let his Pinot G spend so much time in oak.

George's Pinot Gris only gets four to five hours of skin-contact time before sediment gets settled off for fermentation only of the "clear stuff". Once fermentation starts, he keeps the temperature at 13-to-14 degrees Celsius (55-57 degrees Fahrenheit). If it's too cold, the yeast "catches cold" and stops working.

"It's important to get the acid balance right and leave no residual sugar," George said in emphasis.

Given the demand for his wine, and the small amount produced, he suggests people really wanting a bottle should join his mailing list as this receives priority handling.

On our way to the exit, he showed us his notice board with its photos of previous very-much-family-affair harvests. We mentioned how we'd heard of his difficulties with authorities whenever buses drove up.

He admitted being restricted by neighbors' complaints, but, in a way, he appreciates the benefit of having such a limited cellar door, as, now, he can focus more on making the best wine he possibly can.

CHAPTER FIFTEEN: END OF OUR MORNINGTON PENINSULA ADVENTURE

YABBY LAKE

We had a marvelous few days, touring the region, admiring the spectacular scenery, drinking its wonderful wine, enjoying the opportunity to meet many wonderful people who freely shared their love of the grape and were happy to pass on their knowledge to us.

We visited every Cellar Door who responded to our initial requests for access. However, there's one major Pinot G producer in the region that doesn't have a Cellar Door in Australia. Mind you, it does have them in China, the United States, Canada, and the United Kingdom. Being such a large producer, though, its wines are often available in local Australian bottle-shops. With nearly 5 hectares (12 acres) devoted to Pinot gris plantings alone, its production dwarfs that of smaller vineyards, like Paradigm Hill, and Seaforth Estate, that only have small acreages planted. Even the larger Kooyong Estate, only had .2 hectare (.6 acre) of Pinot gris on the vine.

Yabby Lake makes two Pinot Gs (Red Claw and Vineyard Pinot Gris, the latter more expensive), from grapes grown in the duplex sand and clay soils in the sub-district of Moorooduc, similar in terroir to Quealy and Kooyong Estate. According to its website, the main difference between its two wines seems to be from the difference in yield per .4 hectare (1 acre), and the time its grapes are in contact with the lees; the Red Claw being kept for an extra two months.

CHAPTER SIXTEEN: HOME AGAIN, HOME AGAIN!
A TASTING BANQUET

We'd tasted all the wines in situ, but, once home, we sent out invitations to friends and colleagues to join us and provide their opinions on some of the Australian Pinot G wines we'd tasted, plus on a few more. Twenty-three people took us up on our offer.

Simultaneously, we decided to test recipes we thought would go with the wine; if good, they could be included in this book.

Each of our guests was provided a brief background of the Pinot gris grape variety, and was asked for feedback on the wines and foods we provided, especially asked to point out any standout wine or wines, in their opinions.

Dishes were presented in four courses. No attempt was made to do blind trials; instead, guests were given little strips of paper with the wine's name to remind them which wine they were tasting.

THE WINES
From Mornington Peninsula:

Foxeys Hangout late-Pick (a dessert wine)
Kooyong Beurrot Pinot Gris
Quealy's Musk Creek Pinot Gris
Morning Estates (a winery not visited) Pinot Gris
Red Claw Pinot Gris
Red Hill Estate Pinot Grigio
Seaforth Estate Pinot Gris
T'Gallant Juliet
T'Gallant Grace
T'Gallant Imogen
T'Gallant Tribute
Yabby Lake Vineyard

From elsewhere:

Baily & Baily's Monkey's Cousin Pinot Grigio, a Woolworth private label—selling at less than ten dollars a bottle; the antithesis of regional boutique wineries.

Aspen Estate Pinot Grigio, a wine from a mass producer based in the Griffith, Riverina area, a hotter inland region in Australia's irrigation area, with 1,000 hectares (2,471 acres) under vine, a crush capacity of 40,000 tonnes (40,000 US tons), and tank storage for 35,000,000 litres (over 9,000,000 gallons) of wine, whose stated purpose is to "find out what the people want and make it for them. Wine is not for looking at, nor even waxing lyrical about. Wine is for drinking."

Dopff Pinot Gris Reserve, a wine from a long established winery with 70 hectares (173 acres) under vine in the Alsace region of France.

THE FOOD

Starters:

Baked Cauliflower with a Tahini Dipping Sauce served with torn Lebanese bread;
Baked Tofu and Brown Rice patties;
Platter of smoked salmon, celery, carrot nibbles, and camembert with water crackers;
Ricotta and Feta Cheese Puffs made from a traditional Greek recipe (served hot);

T'Gallant's Imogen Pinot Gris was described as sweet and light by some, almost a dessert wine in comparison to the others opened at the same time. This matched its ranking on the Style Spectrum, according to data from the Australian Wine Research Institute. It went particularly well with the tofu and rice patties which were served with a dollop of plain Greek style yogurt on top. Some noted that the slight woodiness in the Gris style didn't go as well with the salmon.

Yabby Lake's Red Claw was definitely drier with a zesty tang which wasn't to everyone's taste, although some said it was enjoyable and palate cleansing. This was judged a better accompaniment to the salmon and the tofu and rice patties.

Mornington Estate (a winery not visited) Pinot Gris

was light, fruity, crisp, and went well with the cauliflower and salmon.

Monkey's Cousin was the stand-out favorite, going particularly well with the smoked salmon and the baked cauliflower, as well as cutting the oiliness of the Tahini dipping sauce.

Entrée (served cold):

Chicken, grape, and asparagus salad
Crab and camembert quiche
Gado Gado, a traditional vegetarian dish from
  Indonesia with a spicy peanut sauce
Smoked Ham and Veal Terrine

T'Gallant Grace went well with the terrine, in that it didn't overpower the flavor. The Imogen also went well with the terrine and with the quiche. Some found the Red Claw good with the terrine because of the way it mellowed the flavor.

Main Course (served hot):

Chicken and spinach pasta bake
Spicy Malaysian vegetable curry puffs
Sweet potato and bacon frittata

Alsace Dopff Pinot Gris definitely hit the spot with drinkers who found it very palatable, dry, clean, good, fruity without being too sweet, and great accompaniment to the curry pasties.

Monkeys Cousin, Yabby Lake Vineyard, and T'Gallant Grace went well with the curry pasties; the latter especially "mild and gentle", according to one guest.

Dessert and Cheese:

Baked chocolate cheesecake with a hint of orange
Lemon cheesecake
Lemon gelato
Platter of sweet rock-melon slices, white grapes and washed rind cheese

Foxeys late-Pick was well received, if not so much in its accompaniment to the sweet chocolate cheesecake than to how brilliantly it matched up with the tart lemon cheesecake, as well as the fruit, and cheese.

Tribute and Musk Creek garnered nice comments with the hot dishes, but were judged better, the next day, with the chocolate cheesecake and the chicken and spinach pasta bake. Seaforth Estate Pinot Gris, which definitely benefited from its couple of years of extra ageing, was very smooth on the palate. The Beurrot was more Griggio than Gris and went well with the cheese and fruit.

NOTE: It was ironic that the most popular wine of the evening was the Baily & Baily Monkeys Cousin. There wasn't much information on the label other than to say it was the produce of South Eastern Australia. Given that it was half the price of the other wines, this demonstrated the difficulties wine producers have in trying to compete with the country's biggest retailer, Woolworths, which owns the biggest liquor chain in the country, Dan Murphys.

PART TWO: SELECTED RECIPES

Baked Cauliflower & *Tahini* Sauce

Half head of cauliflower broken into flowerets. Drizzle with olive oil, arrange on paper covered baking tray and roast in a medium oven until brown.

Sauce:

½ cup *tahini* paste (sesame seed paste)
3 gloves garlic, crushed
2 tblsps. olive oil
¼ cup lemon juice
salt and freshly ground black pepper to taste
2 tblsps. natural yoghurt
1 tblsp. finely chopped continental parsley

Combine crushed garlic and *tahini* paste, add salt to taste. Fold in olive oil and lemon juice. Sauce should be smooth and not too thick add warm water if needed. Mix in chopped parsley. Arrange baked cauliflower on platter with torn up pieces of Lebanese bread and supply sauce in a dipping bowl. The *Tahini* Sauce can be made ahead and stored in an airtight container.

Chicken and Grape Salad

1 barbecue chicken shredded and diced
1 tsp. Dijon mustard
1 cup sour cream
2 tblsps. Pinot G
½ cup of your favorite mayonnaise
5 shallots diced fine
400 g. (1 pound) white grapes (choose small ones if possible)
2 bunches fresh asparagus (dice fine, place in bowl and steep in boiling water for a couple of minutes, then drain)

Mix creamy sauce together, stir in cubed chicken then fold in grapes and asparagus. Season to taste. Serve with lettuce.

Chicken and Spinach Pasta Bake

500 g. (1 pound) chicken thighs or fillets
300 g. (half a pound) ricotta cheese
150 g. (5 ounces) pecorino cheese
200 mls. (1 cup) thickened cream
1 cup chopped baby spinach
150 mls. (½ cup) Pinot G
1 onion chopped finely
1 clove garlic crushed
salt and pepper to taste

1 tsp. dried herbs
500 g. (1 pound) pasta curls

Brown diced chicken in a fry pan or wok, add onion and garlic and cook until the onion is soft. Add wine, herbs and season to taste. Return to the heat for a further five minutes. While the pasta is cooking in a large pan of boiling water, blend the cream and crumbled cheeses until smooth. Remove the chicken mix from pan with a slotted spoon and place in a large casserole dish. Add any remaining juices to the cream and cheese mixture and blend briefly again before folding into the cooked chicken pieces and chopped raw baby spinach. Drain pasta and mix with other ingredients. Cover with a little extra grated pecorino cheese and cook in a moderate oven for twenty-five minutes.

Chocolate and Orange Cheesecake

Pastry Base:

2 cups self-raising flour
1½ tblsps. custard powder
¼ cup castor sugar
pinch of salt
2 tblsps. butter
1 egg
2 tblsps. milk

Filling:

250 g. (1 cup) softened cream cheese
250 g. (1 cup) creamed cottage cheese
½ cup castor (finely-ground) sugar
2 tblsps. chocolate sauce
½ tblsp. grated orange rind
2 eggs

Sift flour, salt, custard powder, castor sugar into bowl. Rub in butter until mixture resembles breadcrumbs. Add combined beaten egg and milk and mix to a firm dough. Chill for fifteen minutes onto a floured surface and knead lightly. Roll out and place into a greased spring-form tin. Prick with a fork and cook for ten minutes at 170 degrees Celsius (350 degrees Fahrenheit), or until it starts to rise.

Have all ingredients for filling at room temperature. Push cottage cheese through a sieve, add cream cheese. Beat the cheeses together, add orange rind and sugar gradually. While base is cooking, add eggs one at a time to cheese mixture, beating in well, finally add the chocolate sauce and stir till all combined. Turn onto cooked crust and return to moderate oven for 35 minutes. Leave in oven until cold.

Topping:

1 carton (1 cup) sour cream
1 tblsp. sugar
1 tsp. vanilla essence

pinch of salt

Mix together and pour on top of chilled cheesecake when cold decorate with peels of chocolate grated from a block of your favorite variety.

Crab and Camembert Quiche

Quantity for 25-cm.- (10-inch-) diameter flan:

350 g. (1½ cups) shredded crab
125 g. (½ cup) camembert
6 large eggs
400 mls. (1½ cups) thickened cream
2 tblsps. plain (all purpose) flour
5 shallots diced fine
freshly ground black pepper
pinch of salt (optional)
2 sheets frozen Puff Pastry

Line quiche dish with frozen puff pastry brought to room temperature. Drain crab and arrange on bottom. Slice camembert and shallots finely and arrange on top. Whisk eggs, cream, pepper, and pour on top.

Place quiche dish on metal tray and put into hot oven for ten minutes. Lower heat to moderate for fifty minutes. Let stand and while cooling, run blunt knife around edge of flan tin, easing pastry away from side and carefully lifting. As quiche cools, it will shrink and then be easier to serve.

Curried Vegetable Puffs
(with thanks to Kim for her traditional Malaysian recipe)

Filling:

3 large potatoes cubed
2 tblsps. olive oil
1 large brown onion chopped
3 cloves garlic chopped
½ red capsicum seeded and chopped
1 tblsp. Malaysian Curry powder
1 tblsp. Tom Yum (a Thai curry paste found in Asian grocery stores—sourish and tasty)
1 tblsp. soy sauce
3 tsps. sugar (or alternative for Diabetics)
½ cup skim milk

Pastry:

3 sheets puff pastry cut into 9 round shapes.

Boil potatoes until soft. Heat oil in a medium-sized pot, add garlic, fry until golden, add onion, fry until golden, add capsicum. Add Tom Yum paste and curry powder, fry until aromatic. Stir in the soy sauce, sugar and milk. Mix in cooked potatoes. Allow to cool

Heat oven to 180 degrees Celsius (350 degrees Fahrenheit), slightly less if fan-forced. Place one teaspoon of filling onto round shaped pastry and fold into half. Pinch the edges. Arrange curry puffs on lightly floured or paper lined tray and bake for thirty minutes or until golden brown.

Gado Gado

½ cabbage shredded fine
1 cucumber sliced paper thin
bean sprouts
4 medium potatoes, boiled, peeled and diced
4 eggs (whisked and cooked like omelet then sliced)
100 g. (½ cup) tofu fried and diced (optional)

Arrange vegetables on top of lettuce

Peanut Sauce:

300 g. (1 cup) crunchy peanut butter
410 mls. (1½ cups) coconut milk (approximate)

Mix peanut butter with small amount of water and shake in a closed container gradually adding coconut milk until pourable. Put into saucepan.

Add chili powder to taste
2 tblsps. brown sugar
1 tblsps. balsamic vinegar
1 tsp. cumin
½ tsp. All Spice

Stir until over low heat until all combined, add water or coconut milk to required consistency. Pour into jug and serve beside vegetables.

Lemon Marmalade Cheesecake

Base:

155 g. (8 oz.) plain sweet biscuits
75 g. (3 tblsps.) melted butter

Line side of 21-cm. (8-inch) spring-form tin with baking paper. Crush or process biscuits until they are like fine breadcrumbs. Add melted butter until just combined. Using one hand, press crumb mixture evenly on base only of tin. Cover and refrigerate for thirty minutes or until firm.

Filling:

500 g. (2 cups) softened cream cheese
300 mls. (just over 1 cup) thickened cream
1 cup of lemon juice
1 tsp. lemon zest
1 tblsp. gelatin
400 g. (1½ cup) can of sweetened condensed milk

Stir 100-150 mls. (about half a cup) of gelatin into about half a cup of hot water and mix to dissolve fully. In food processor, blend condensed milk, cream, softened cream cheese, lemon juice and lemon zest. Add dissolved gelatin and blend until smooth. Pour mixture onto base, cover and refrigerate. When nearly set add topping:

Topping:

3 limes
2 tblsps. sugar
2 tblsps. corn flour

Remove zest of three limes in strips and reserve until end. Mix corn flour with a small amount of water, make up to same volume as juice from limes and place in saucepan over low heat. Add two tablespoons of sugar and stir until sugar is dissolved and mixture thickens. Allow to cool slightly before spreading over top of cheesecake mixture. Decorate with zest strips and refrigerate until serving.

Ricotta or Feta Cheese Puffs

500 g. (2 cups) ricotta cheese
200 g. (1 cup) sheep and goat's milk feta cheese
1 egg
2 tblsps. dried bread crumbs
sprig of chopped continental parsley
1 tblsp. flour
sheets of frozen puff pastry

Crumble cheeses and mix ingredients together until smooth. Cut each sheet of pastry into nine. Place one teaspoonful of mixture on each and fold edges over crimping them together. Arrange on baking sheets on tray and cook in a moderate oven for twenty-five minutes or until pastry is golden brown. Puffs can be prepared ahead of time and frozen until just before cooking and serving.

Sweet Potato and Zucchini Frittata

1 sweet potato, peeled, cubed and baked on baking paper covered dish in oven until cooked.
200 g. (1 cup) bacon, diced
1 onion finely chopped
8 eggs
200 g. (1 cup) feta cheese crumbled
300 mls. (1 cup) thickened cream
2 zucchinis grated
1 tblsp. chopped fresh oregano
ground pepper
½ cup grated vintage cheese as topping

Dice sweet potato and spread across the bottom of a casserole dish lined with baking paper. Place in a hot oven for fifteen minutes or until soft. While this is cooking, brown bacon in a fry pan and when nearly cooked add finely chopped onion. Spread over cooked sweet potato. Add layer of crumbled feta and oregano. Add layer of grated raw zucchini. Whip eggs and cream, add pepper to taste. Pour over vegetables, and top with grated cheese. Cook in moderate oven for at least fifty minutes until golden brown on top.

Tofu and Rice Patties

½ cup brown rice (uncooked)
½ cup rolled oats
1 sprig fresh or 1 tsp. dried thyme
1 tsp. cumin
150 g. (½ cup) silken tofu
2 cloves garlic crushed
1 tblsp. rich Japanese soy sauce
2 tblsps. tomato puree
2 tsps. Dijon mustard
3 shallots finely chopped
½ cup grated carrot
½ cup grated celery
⅛ cup sesame seeds
Greek style yoghurt
olive oil

Cook brown rice while preparing other ingredients. Combine in a mixing bowl other ingredients except olive oil and yoghurt. Drain cooked brown rice and combine with the mixing bowl ingredients. Line a baking tray and brush with olive oil. Place mixture on baking tray. Smooth to a thickness of 1 cm. (½ inch). Brush top with olive oil. Cook in a preheated oven for twenty minutes at 200 degrees Celsius (400 degrees Fahrenheit), until mixture firms before browning. Remove from oven and rest for a few minutes for mixture to set. Cut into bite-sized pieces and place a small dollop of Greek yogurt on top of each piece for serving.

Veal and Smoked Ham Terrine

1 kg. (2 pounds) veal steaks
250 g. (½ pound) thinly sliced smoked ham
bacon to line the terrine dish
1 tblsp. chopped parsley.
1 tblsp. chopped onion.
2 tblsps. chopped fresh oregano
dash of brandy
1 cup of Pinot G

Pound the veal into thin sheets. Line the terrine dish with bacon rashers and strew with parsley and onion. Overlay the bottom layer of bacon with pounded veal and season with chopped oregano. Add a layer of smoked ham. Continue to add layers of parsley and onion, veal, oregano and ham. Add a dash of brandy on top and then pour wine over the meat layers until the crevices are filled with liquid. Place terrine dish in a larger pan of hot water and cook in oven for about two hours at 160 degrees Celsius (320 degrees Fahrenheit). As soon as the meat is removed from oven, cover with heavy foil and weight done the meat layers with a brick (or something of similar weight). When fully cooled, thinly slice the terrine for serving.

ABOUT THE AUTHORS

A. B. GAYLE, while preparing to write a historical novel, based on the life of a New Zealand missionary, was diverted into writing science fiction and, then, romances. Her adult e-books, *Mardi Gras* and *Caught*, have received critical acclaim. When not writing, she professionally edits the works of other writers, interviews her fellow authors, writes book reviews, and, most recently, writes about and drinks wine.

She can be found on her website:

http://www.abgayle.com

WILLIAM MALTESE is a long-time wine connoisseur, and author of *William Maltese's Wine Taster's Diary: Spokane/Pullman Washington Wine Region,* and (with Bonnie Clark) of the bestselling *Back of the Boat Gourmet Cooking,* and (with Adrienne Z. Milligan) of the bestselling *The Gluten-Free Way: My Way*—all for the Borgo Press Imprint of Wildside Press. He's traveled much of the world, drinking good wine and eating good food at each and every opportunity. He has finally decided to put down some of his thoughts, and those of his friends, on fine wining and dining into *THE TRAVELING GOURMAND* series books for Wildside Press. He's also been honored with a listing in the prestigious *Who's Who in America*. For more information on William, please check out his websites:

http://www.williammaltese.com
http://www.facebook.com/williammaltese
http://www.facebook.com/flickerwarriors
http://www.facebook.com/draqual
http://www.myspace.com/williammaltese
http://www.myspace.com/maltesecandlegallery
http://www.theglutenfreewaymyway.com
http://www.myspace.com/draqual
http://www.myspace.com/flickerwarriors

(for Xocai® Chocolates):

http://www.mxi.myvoffice.com/williammaltese

www.ingramcontent.com/pod-product-compliance
Lightning Source LLC
Chambersburg PA
CBHW031957080426
42735CB00007B/422